*Enjoy!!*
☺ *Linda*

# Quick Soups 'n Salads

## A ONE FOOT IN THE KITCHEN COOKBOOK

Written and Compiled by
CYNDI DUNCAN AND GEORGIE PATRICK

Illustrated by
COLETTE McLAUGHLIN

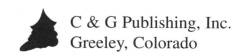 C & G Publishing, Inc.
Greeley, Colorado

# Quick Soups 'n Salads

Copyright © 1999
by Cyndi Duncan and Georgie Patrick

Library of Congress Catalog Card Number: 99-93362
ISBN 0-9626335-7-7
Printed in the United States of America

Illustrations and photograph by Colette McLaughlin
Graphic Design by Gregory Effinger, for
Colorado Independent Graphics, Advertising and Reproduction, www.cigargraphics.com

*Nutrition analysis has been calculated on Mastercook II software.*

*To the best of our knowledge, all information included in this book is correct and complete. The publisher and authors offer no guarantees and disclaim any liability attributed to its use.*

Published by C & G Publishing, Inc.
P.O. Box 5199
Greeley, Colorado 80634-0103
For orders and information:  (800) 925-3172

To the Georgies and the Cyndis of the world

who are ageless, or pretend they are

who enjoy the mornings, and to those who don't

who have brain freezes without eating ice cream

who are finally ready for a housekeeper, but still won't hire one

who now have albums for the photos previously in 35 year old shoe boxes

and who are surprised the year 2000 has arrived

this book's for you!

# Contents

# Introduction

After *Quick Crockery Cooking* and *Quick Mexican Cooking* became award winning books we decided to continue the quick cooking saga of the Cyndis and Georgies of the world with the creation of *Quick Soups 'n Salads*, third in the "one foot in the kitchen" series. This was an easy choice since we both are soup and salad people, and these soups and salads are easy to prepare. Our purpose in writing these user-friendly cookbooks is to make cooking fun, creative and, above all, easy. We want you in and out of the kitchen in a hurry. Just have someone else do the dishes.

Our Queen of Easy, Georgie, still reigns and admittedly, some easy has rubbed off on me. I didn't ever dream I'd be opening cans and slitting freezer bags in my kitchen. Now I know why Georgie can't cook without kitchen shears. She tells me to, "Hide the evidence; who will know?" And you know, she's right again, (darn it!).

Okay, now Georgie has me admitting that I take a few shortcuts, but give me a day in the kitchen and I'm happy. She, on the other hand, has never expressed a burning desire to spend a day in the kitchen cooking up a storm. She would rather find a quiet spot, where no one can find her, and read. She's one of the few people who can have three or four novels going at once and still know what each of them is about. Sometimes I have to give her a day off so she can finish at least one of them.

In spite of our differences, we are both committed to helping you prepare quick, nutritious meal that will get you rave reviews and keep you out of the kitchen.

*Quick Soups 'n Salads* lets the Cyndis of this world chop to their hearts content and the Georgies snip away with their kitchen shears . . . perfect for our busy lifestyles.

*Cyndi*

# Soups

# BEEF BROTH

*Make your own broth occasionally to use in recipes that call for beef broth. Add one or two beef bouillon cubes and serve as au jus for beef sandwiches.*

4 pounds beef soup bones, cut in pieces
1 cup onion, sliced
1/2 cup celery, chopped
8 whole peppercorns
2 teaspoons parsley
2 teaspoons salt
1 bay leaf
5 cups water
Salt and pepper to taste

In large pan, combine all ingredients. Cover and simmer at least 4 hours (in slow cooker, 12 hours). Remove bones. Strain broth into large bowl through cheesecloth. Refrigerate. When ready to use, remove fat that has formed on top. Add salt and pepper. Remove meat from bones and save for another meal. Makes 4 cups beef stock and about 2 cups cooked meat.

*Per serving: 153 calories; 8.8 fat grams*

 To clarify broth, crush egg shell with 1 egg white and 1/4 cup water. Add to hot stock. Bring to boiling. Remove from heat and let stand 5 minutes; strain through cheesecloth.

# Footnotes from Cyndi and Georgie

Quick Soups 'n Salads, like our other "one foot in the kitchen" cookbooks, features quick and easy recipes with ingredients that are usually found in your kitchen. We strive to prepare healthy meals but, like most cooks, occasionally give in to old cravings. We know you have favorite recipes that often keep you in your kitchen when you should be enjoying time with family and friends. So, we have provided hints to make your meals easier to prepare and more nutritious.

Include texture, color, balance of flavors and a pleasing presentation to create interesting, appealing and delicious meals.

Use skim milk and cut the amount of cheese in half to reduce calories by 35 and fat by 3 grams.

Dietary information is based on one cup servings. Adjust the recipe accordingly.

Cream based soups are best when prepared just before serving. Boiling milk/cream based soups will cause curdling.

One bouillon cube or 1 tablespoon granules dissolved in one cup of water is equal to one cup of broth. A 16-ounce can of broth equals about 2 cups.

To make a low sodium soup, reduce salt or use salt substitute.

Brown and drain meat before adding vegetables. The vegetables will absorb more grease from the meat if cooked with the meat before draining.

Cutting lettuce with knife will cause rusting. It is best to tear into pieces or use a plastic utensil. It is personal preference as to whether to choose firm heads or softer heads of lettuce. Softer heads have more dark green leaves and, in Cyndi's opinion, become crisper with refrigeration. When selecting lettuce, smell the core. If it smells strong, the lettuce will be bitter. This method hasn't failed Georgie yet. Wash and core lettuce under cool running water. Pat dry with kitchen towel or paper towel.

Some recipes list either salad dressing or mayonnaise. It is purely personal preference. Just a note: light salad dressing has more calories than light mayonnaise.

The oil listed in the recipes is vegetable oil, and the vinegar is white, unless otherwise stated.

# Notes:

# CHICKEN BROTH

*Make your own and substitute in any recipe that calls for canned chicken broth or bouillon cubes.*

3 pounds bony chicken pieces (or use 3-4 chicken breasts)
1 large onion, quartered
3 whole cloves
3 stalks celery with leaves, cut up
1 carrot, quartered
1 1/2 teaspoons salt
1/4 teaspoon pepper
4 cups water

If desired, discard fat and skin from chicken pieces. In large pan, place all ingredients. Bring to boil; reduce heat and simmer 4 hours (if using slow cooker, cook on low for 8-10 hours). Remove chicken and vegetables with slotted spoon. Strain broth into large bowl through cheesecloth. Refrigerate. When ready to use, remove fat that has formed on top. Refrigerate in covered container. Makes 4-5 cups chicken broth.

*Per serving: 174 calories; 7.2 fat grams*

 To clarify, refer to footnote that follows Beef Stock recipe on previous page.

# EASY CONSOMME

*The vegetables make this a colorful base starter for soups, or serve it alone as a starter for a meal.*

2 10-ounce cans condensed chicken broth
1 2/3 cups water
1/2 cup carrot, shredded
1/4 cup green pepper, finely chopped
1/4 cup green onion, finely chopped

In medium saucepan, combine call ingredients. Heat to boiling. Serve hot. Serves 8 as starter.

*Per serving: 29 calories; 0.8 fat grams*

 Consomme can be used in place of broth.

# VELVET AVOCADO SOUP

*Serve cold as an appetizer in demitasse cups or as a side course in shallow soup bowls.*

2 avocados, pitted, peeled and mashed
3 cups chicken stock (homemade, if
   available)
1 tablespoon green onions, chopped
Juice of 1/2 lime
Few drops hot red pepper sauce
Salt and white pepper to taste
4 tablespoons sour cream
4 tablespoons salsa

In food processor or blender, mix all ingredients, except sour cream and salsa. Chill until ready to serve. Garnish each serving with dollops of sour cream and salsa. Serves 4.

*Per serving: 188 calories; 16.1 fat grams*

# B.L.T. SOUP

8 slices bacon, cut into pieces
Bacon grease
1/2 head lettuce, chopped
3 tablespoons flour
4 cups milk (can use 2 cups cream and 2
    cups water)
4 fresh tomatoes, chopped
Pinch cayenne pepper
Salt and pepper to taste
1/4 teaspoon sage

In large pan, cook bacon pieces to desired crispness. Do not drain. Add lettuce to bacon; cook 4-5 minutes. Add flour and stir. Add milk and stir constantly until thickened. Carefully stir in tomatoes, cayenne, salt, pepper and sage. Heat to serving temperature; do not boil. Ladle into soup bowls. Serves 4-6.

*Per serving: 225 calories; 16.0 fat grams*

# MEXICAN RICE AND BEAN SOUP

*Easy to prepare; cook in slow cooker for a quick meal after a long day at the office.*

1/2 cup onion, chopped
1/3 cup green pepper, chopped
1 clove garlic, minced
1 tablespoon oil
1 4-ounce package sliced dried beef, cut
    in strips
1 18-ounce can tomato juice
1 15-ounce can red kidney beans
1 1/2 cups water
1/2 cup rice
1 teaspoon paprika
3/4 teaspoon chili powder
1/2 teaspoon salt
1/4 teaspoon pepper

In large pan, cook onion, garlic in oil 3 minutes. Add remaining ingredients. Stir to mix. Cover and cook 45 minutes (If using slow cooker, cook on low 6 hours). Stir again before serving. Serves 6.

*Per serving: 427 calories; 6.4 fat grams*

# BABY LIMA BEAN SOUP

*Quick and easy to assemble; great candidate for the slow cooker. Georgie and Cyndi love being served this soup by Cyndi's mom after a long day at a trade show.*

1 6-ounce package baby lima or navy beans
5 cups boiling water
1 1/2 cups celery, chopped
2 onions, chopped
1 large hamhock

Boil beans in water 10 minutes. Add celery, onion and hamhock. Simmer over low heat at least 4 hours. Remove hamhock. Option: Place in slow cooker and simmer on low 6-10 hours. Serves 8.

*Per serving: 112 calories; 2.4 fat grams*

Chop up meat from hamhock and put back in soup or use meat for sandwiches.

# QUICK BLACK BEAN SOUP

4 slices bacon, cooked and crumbled
2 tablespoons bacon drippings
1 large onion, chopped
1 clove garlic, minced
2 15-ounce cans undrained black beans
1 14-ounce can beef broth
1 1/4 cups water
3/4 cup salsa
1/2 teaspoon salt
1/8 teaspoon oregano
8 teaspoons light sour cream

In medium saucepan, combine onion, garlic and bacon drippings. Cook 3 minutes. Add beans, broth, water, picante sauce, salt and oregano. Cover and simmer 20 minutes. Ladle into soup bowls. Top with dollop of sour cream and bacon. Serve extra salsa on the side. Serves 6-8.

*Per serving: 512 calories; 9.7 fat grams*

# BLACK BEAN AND HAM SOUP

2 15-ounce cans black beans
8 cups water
1 1/2 cups lean ham, cubed
2 stalks celery with leaves, sliced
1 onion, chopped
2 bay leaves
1/2 teaspoon dry mustard
2 teaspoons sugar
2 teaspoons salt
1/2 teaspoon pepper
1 teaspoon lime juice
Few drops hot pepper sauce
Parmesan cheese

In large pan, combine all ingredients. Bring to boil; reduce heat. Cover and simmer 30 minutes. Ladle into soup bowls and garnish with parmesan cheese. Serves 10.

*Per serving: 144 calories; 1.5 fat grams*

 Substitute leftover turkey, beef, pork or shrimp for the ham.

# BLACK-EYED PEA SOUP

*A traditional soup often served on New Years Eve for good luck.*

2 slices bacon, cooked crisp, broken in
    small pieces
1 tablespoon bacon drippings
2 tablespoons flour
1 small onion, chopped
1/4 cup green pepper, chopped
1 15-ounce can black-eyed peas
6 cups water
3/4 teaspoon salt
1/8 teaspoon pepper
1/2 teaspoon garlic salt

In medium pan, combine bacon drippings, flour, onion and green pepper; saute 5 minutes. Add remaining ingredients; heat to simmering. Serve with parmesan toast or cornbread. Serves 6.

*Per serving: 285 calories; 4.2 fat grams*

# GENEVA'S BLACK-EYED PEA SOUP

2 16-ounce cans black-eyed peas with
    green beans
1 16-ounce can water
1 stalk celery, diced
1/2 onion, diced
1/2 green pepper
1/2 red pepper
1/2 pound smoked sausage, diced
1 teaspoon parsley
1/4 teaspoon oregano
Salt and pepper to taste

In large pan, combine peas and beans, water, celery, onion and peppers. Bring to boil. Add remaining ingredients and simmer 20-30 minutes. Ladle into soup bowls. Serves 6.

*Per serving: 550 calories; 11.5 fat grams*

# LENTIL AND MUSHROOM SOUP

2 15-ounce cans condensed lentil soup
2 cups water
2 cups dry white wine
1/3 cup dark molasses
1 onion, chopped
1 stalk celery, chopped
1 clove garlic, minced
1/2 teaspoon salt
2 bay leaves
5 strips bacon, cooked crisp, crumbled
2 tablespoons butter
4 cups fresh mushrooms, quartered
1/3 cup green onions, chopped

In large pan, combine soup, water, wine, molasses, onion, celery, garlic, salt and bay leaves. Bring to boil and simmer 15 minutes. In small skillet, melt butter; saute bacon and mushrooms 5 minutes. Remove from heat. About 10 minutes before serving, add bacon and mushrooms to soup mixture. Ladle into soup bowls. Garnish with green onions. Serves 6.

*Per serving: 341 calories; 7.0 fat grams*

# QUICK BROCCOLI SOUP

*This soup is easy to prepare on camping trips.*

2-3 tablespoons light margarine
1 small onion, diced
1/2 cup celery, sliced
2 cloves garlic
1 1/2 cups broccoli, sliced
1 1/2 cups water
2 10-ounce cans cream of celery soup
1 cup lowfat milk
Salt and pepper to taste
1/2 cup white cheddar cheese, cubed

In medium saucepan, combine margarine, onion, celery and garlic. Saute 3-4 minutes. Add broccoli and water; simmer 5 minutes. Add soup and milk. Stir until smooth. Heat to boiling. Season with salt and pepper. Add cheese; stir. Serve immediately. Serves 4.

*Per serving: 163 calories; 8.0 fat grams*

# BROCCOLI CHEESE SOUP

*This soup recipe is a favorite from our Quick Crockery Cooking cookbook.*

1 large head broccoli, washed and chopped
2 cups water
4 chicken bouillon cubes
2 cups milk
1/4-1/2 cup flour
1/2 cup half and half or evaporated milk
2 cups American cheese, cubed

In large pan, combine broccoli, water and bouillon cubes. Simmer 15 minutes. In small bowl, mix milk and flour together. Slowly pour into broccoli mixture, stirring until thickened. Reduce heat. Add half and half and cheese. Stir until cheese is melted. Ladle into soup bowls. Serves 6.

*Per serving: 248 calories; 17.1 fat grams*

Foot Note: Substitute 1 10-ounce package frozen broccoli to save time.

# EASY FRENCH ONION SOUP

1 1/2 teaspoons olive oil
2 large yellow onions, thinly sliced
1/4 teaspoon thyme
2 cups water
2 cloves garlic
2 1/2 teaspoons flour
1 cup beef broth or 1 bouillon cube dis-
    solved in 1 cup boiling water
1/2 teaspoon nutmeg
4 slices French bread, toasted
2 tablespoons Swiss cheese, grated
4 tablespoons parmesan cheese

In large skillet, cook oil, onions, thyme and 1 table-spoon water 5 minutes. Reduce heat; add garlic and saute 1 minute. Add flour; cook 2 minutes. Stir in broth, remaining water and nutmeg. Bring to boil; skim off foam. Reduce heat, cover and simmer 30 minutes. Preheat boiler. Place 4 heatproof bowls on baking sheet. Ladle soup into bowls, top with toast and sprinkle with cheese and parmesan. Broil 1 minute. Serve immediately. Serves 4.

*Per serving: 149 calories; 4.8 fat grams*

 Foot Note: Easy Onion Soup: Use 3 15-ounce cans beef broth or leftover broth from a roast. Combine with 3 large onions and salt and pepper to taste. Simmer until onions are tender. Can be topped with bread and cheeses.

# CREAM OF BROCCOLI SOUP

*A friend, Margaret, shared this delicately flavored favorite with us. Great at the beginning of a meal or served with a sandwich or salad.*

6 cups water
1 10-ounce package frozen chopped broccoli
3/4 cup onion, finely chopped
1 teaspoon salt
1 teaspoon seasoned salt
2 teaspoons white pepper
1 teaspoon garlic powder
2 cups mild cheddar cheese, shredded
1 cup milk
1 cup cream
1/4 cup butter
1/3 cup flour
1/2 cup cold water

In 3-quart saucepan, bring 6 cups water to a boil; add broccoli and onion. Boil 10-12 minutes. Add seasonings. Gradually add cheese, stirring constantly until cheese melts. Add milk, cream and butter; stir and heat to boiling. In separate bowl, mix flour and water, stirring until mixture is smooth. Stir slowly into hot mixture. Lower heat and cook until soup is consistency of heavy cream. Serves 8-10.

*Per serving: 258 calories; 21.1 fat grams*

# VERMONT CHEESE SOUP

4 large carrots, chopped
1 large onion, chopped
1 large green pepper, chopped
3-4 stalks celery, chopped
8 cups water
1 stick butter
1/2 cup flour
1/2 teaspoon pepper
2 cups half and half
1/2 pound cheddar cheese, shredded

In large pan, combine carrots, onion, pepper, celery and water. Bring to boiling, reduce heat and simmer for 15 minutes. In small pan, melt butter. Stir in flour and mix well. Add to vegetable mixture, stirring constantly until thickened. Add pepper, milk and cheese, stirring constantly until cheese is melted. Do not boil. Bring to serving temperature. Ladle into bowl; garnish with chives or chopped black olives. Serves 8.

*Per serving: 346 calories; 27.9 fat grams*

# CARROT AND CREAM CHEESE SOUP

2 1/2 cups chicken broth
4 cups (2 pounds) peeled and sliced carrots
1/2 cup onion, chopped
3/4 teaspoon caraway seed
1 8-ounce package light cream cheese, cut
    in half lengthwise, then sliced crosswise
1/3 cup carrot, shredded

Reserve 4 slices of cream cheese for garnish. In large pan, combine broth, carrots, onion and 1/2 teaspoon caraway seed; bring to boil. Reduce heat and simmer 15 minutes. Spoon broth and carrots into blender or food processor and whirl until smooth. Return to pan. Stir over medium heat to boiling. Add cheese and whisk mixture until smooth. Ladle soup into bowls; top with reserved cream cheese and remaining caraway seed. Serves 4.

*Per serving: 223 calories; 11.9 fat grams*

# CAULIFLOWER AU GRATIN SOUP

2 onions, sliced
4 tablespoons butter
2 teaspoons caraway seeds
2 10-ounce cans chicken broth
1 head cauliflower, thinly sliced
2 teaspoons lemon juice
1/2 cup processed cheese, cubed
Salt and pepper to taste
2 Roma tomatoes, seeded and chopped

In medium pan, saute onions in butter 5 minutes, stirring often. Add caraway seeds, broth and cauliflower; simmer 15 minutes. Pour mixture into blender; whirl to puree mixture. Return mixture to pan. Add lemon juice, salt and pepper; stir and heat to simmering. Add cheese and stir constantly until melted. Extra broth can be added to make desired consistency. Ladle into soup bowls and garnish with tomatoes. Serves 4.

*Per serving: 230 calories; 17.7 fat grams*

# CAJUN CORN AND SAUSAGE SOUP

1 onion, chopped
1 green pepper, chopped
6 green onions, sliced
2 tablespoons oil
1/4 cup potato flakes
3 cups water
1 15-ounce can Cajun-style stewed tomatoes
2 tomatoes, chopped
1 6-ounce can tomato paste
2 16-ounce packages frozen corn
3 cups cooked ham, cubed
1 1/2 pounds fully cooked smoked sausage,
    sliced
1/8 teaspoon cayenne pepper
Salt to taste
Hot pepper sauce to taste

In large pan, saute onion, green pepper and green onions in oil 5 minutes. Add potato flakes and water; stir until thickened. Add remaining ingredients. Simmer uncovered 40 minutes, stirring occasionally. Serves 12.

*Per serving: 409 calories; 23.7 fat grams*

If necessary, add more potato flakes for a thicker soup.

# QUICK CHEESY CORN CHOWDER

1 large potato, diced
1 large onion, chopped
1/4 cup carrots, diced
1/4 cup celery, diced
1 cup frozen corn, thawed
1 cup water
1 15-ounce can chicken broth
2 tablespoons parsley
1 cup cheddar cheese, grated
1/2 cup half and half cream

In large pan, combine all ingredients, except cheese and cream. Simmer 15 minutes. Add cheese and cream; stir until cheese is melted. Do not boil. Serves 3-4.

*Per serving: 255 calories; 14.6 fat grams*

If you like beer cheese soup, substitute beer for water and omit corn. Pour into blender; whirl until smooth. Return to heat.

# SPLIT PEA SOUP

*This soup is quick and easy to assemble; peas do not require soaking. However, cooking the peas does require a little extra time, so we recommend using your slow cooker.*

1 pound yellow or green dry split peas,
    washed and sorted
8 cups hot water
1 1/2 to 2 pounds hamhock
3/4 cup onion, minced
1 cup celery, finely diced
1 cup carrots, peeled, finely diced
1 bay leaf
1/2 garlic salt
1/4 teaspoon thyme
Salt to taste
Freshly ground pepper to taste

In large pan, bring peas and water to boiling; simmer 30 minutes with lid tilted. Add remaining ingredients, except salt and pepper. Simmer on low heat 30 minutes, stirring occasionally. Remove bone, cut off meat and dice. Return to soup mixture. Season with salt and pepper. Ladle into soup bowls. Serves 6-8.

*Per serving: 358 calories; 9.8 fat grams*

# RED PEPPER SOUP

*Serve this soup hot or cold.*

5 red peppers, sliced
1 medium onion, chopped
1/4 cup butter
2 20-ounce cans chicken broth
1/2 cup half and half
2 teaspoons brown sugar
Salt and pepper to taste
1/2 cup fresh mushrooms, chopped

In medium pan, combine peppers, onion and butter; saute 5 minutes. Add broth and simmer 15 minutes. Pour into blender and whirl until smooth. Pour back into pan. Add cream, sugar, salt and pepper. Ladle into soup bowls; garnish with mushrooms. Serves 6.

*Per serving: 178 calories; 12.0 fat grams*

Foot Note

This soup is an excellent source of vitamin C. Red peppers contain more vitamin C by weight than citrus fruits.

# POTATO SOUP

*This soup is a Christmas Eve favorite for our friend Sheryl's family.*

2 10-ounce cans condensed chicken broth
1 10-ounce can condensed beef broth
3 cups water
2 large onions, diced
4 large potatoes, peeled, diced
2 cups celery, sliced
1 8-ounce can sliced mushrooms, drained
1/3 cup butter or margarine
1/3 cup flour
Salt and pepper to taste
1/2 cup parsley, dried or fresh
2 cups Swiss cheese, shredded

In large pan, combine broth, water, onions, potatoes, celery and mushrooms. Cover and simmer 30 minutes. In small skillet, melt butter; add flour. Stir constantly over medium heat until mixture becomes golden brown. Add to simmering soup. Stir constantly until soup bubbles and thickens. Season with salt, pepper and parsley. Ladle into soup bowls; top with generous amounts of Swiss cheese. Serves 8.

*Per serving: 287 calories; 16.9 fat grams*

**Foot Note** If butter and flour mixture is lumpy or stiff, stir in 1 cup of the simmering broth until smooth. Slowly add mixture to soup, stirring constantly.

# LEEK AND POTATO SOUP

2 chicken bouillon cubes
2 cups boiling water
3 large potatoes, diced
2 1/2 cups leeks, chopped, white part only
2 tablespoons onion, chopped
1/2 cup milk
Salt and pepper to taste
Chives, optional

In medium pan, dissolve bouillon in boiling water. Add potatoes, leeks and onion. Simmer on low heat 30 minutes. (If you want a smooth soup, run it through blender and return it to pan.) Add milk, salt and pepper. Heat. Ladle into soup bowls and top with chives. Serves 4.

*Per serving: 96 calories; 1.3 fat grams*

 Dill bread is a delicious compliment to this soup.

# POTATO AND HAM SOUP

*A quick way to use leftover ham and mashed potatoes.*

1/4 cup celery, chopped
2 tablespoons onion flakes
1 teaspoon chives, chopped
2 tablespoons butter
2 cups milk
1 1/2 cups mashed potatoes
1 chicken bouillon cube or 1 teaspoon
    bouillon granules
1 cup lean leftover, cooked ham
1 teaspoon parsley

In large saucepan, cook celery, onion and chives in butter 5 minutes. Add milk, mashed potatoes and bouillon. Blend until smooth. Stir in ham and parsley. Bring almost to boiling. Reduce heat and simmer 20 minutes, stirring occasionally. Do not boil. Serves 4.

*Per serving: 256 calories; 12.7 fat grams*

Leftover mashed potatoes can be frozen. Thaw and mix them with an egg, salt and pepper. Shape into patties and cook in skillet with butter, browning on both sides. Serve as a side dish at breakfast or dinner.

# SPINACH POTATO SOUP

3-4 potatoes, peeled, diced
1 1/2 cups water
1 tablespoon onion, chopped
1 teaspoon chicken bouillon granules, or 1
    chicken bouillon cube
1/2 teaspoon garlic salt
1 cup fresh or frozen spinach, finely
    chopped
1 cup heavy cream
1/4 teaspoon nutmeg

In large pan, combine potatoes, water, onion and bouillon; bring to boil. Cook 10 minutes. Add remaining ingredients and cook 15 minutes until spinach is tender. Serves 4.

*Per serving: 276 calories; 22.3 fat grams*

 Puree this soup until smooth. Serve cold as a starter for Holiday or St. Patrick's Day meal.

# LEFTOVER BAKED POTATO CHILI

1 pound lean ground beef
1 onion, chopped
1 clove garlic, minced
4 tablespoons chili powder
1/4 cup salsa
1 15-ounce can ranch-style beans
1 15-ounce can Mexican style tomatoes
1 15-ounce can tomato sauce
2 baked potatoes, diced
1/2 cup shredded cheddar cheese
1/2 cup tortilla chips, crushed

In large pan, brown ground beef; drain. Add onion, garlic, chili powder and salsa. Cover and simmer 5 minutes. Add beans, tomatoes, tomato sauce and potatoes. Stir and simmer 30 minutes. Ladle into soup bowls. Top with cheese and tortilla chips. Serves 8.

*Per serving: 547 calories; 20.2 fat grams*

Foot Note

Always bake extra potatoes for use in casseroles, other soups or as hash-browns. Or, if you have none on hand, microwave a potato on high 4 minutes, turning after 2 minutes.

# CURRIED SWEET POTATO AND ZUCCHINI SOUP

*Use as a starter to your favorite seafood dinner.*

1 leek (white portion only), sliced
1 medium carrot, sliced
3 tablespoons light butter or margarine
2 sweet potatoes, peeled and cubed
2 16-ounce cans chicken broth
3 medium zucchini, sliced (do not peel)
1 teaspoon salt
1/2 teaspoon curry powder
1/4 teaspoon white pepper
1/4 cup light sour cream
2 tablespoons lowfat milk
Dash curry powder
Paprika

In large pan, saute leeks and carrots in butter 5 minutes stirring occasionally. Add sweet potatoes, broth, zucchini, salt, curry powder and pepper. Bring to boil. Reduce heat; cover and simmer 30 minutes. Carefully spoon small portions into blender and puree until coarsely blended. Remove to another large pan or bowl; repeat until all is blended. Return to heat; do not boil. Simmer 3-4 minutes. Mix sour cream, milk and curry. Ladle soup into small soup bowls and drizzle with sour cream mixture. Sprinkle with paprika. Serves 10.

*Per serving: 51 calories; 2.0 fat grams*

# CREAM OF PUMPKIN SOUP

*Our friend, Barbara, shared this recipe with us.*

4 cups pumpkin (1 medium fresh pumpkin
    or 2 15-ounce cans pumpkin)
3 carrots, sliced
3 stalks celery, sliced
1 onion, chopped
1 bay leaf
3 15-ounce cans chicken or vegetable broth
1 cup evaporated milk
1/2 teaspoon nutmeg
1 tablespoon honey
Salt and freshly ground pepper to taste

In large pan, combine pumpkin, carrots, celery, onion, bay leaf and broth. Bring to boil, lower heat and cover. If using fresh pumpkin, simmer 1 hour. If using canned pumpkin, simmer 15-20 minutes. Remove from heat. Mash or run through blender until smooth. Return to pan and add remaining ingredients. Add extra milk to adjust consistency, if needed. Serves 10-12.

*Per serving: 93 calories; 3.1 fat grams*

 Use leftover cold soup as a dip for chips. Serve in small hollowed out pumpkin for an unusual presentation at a party.

# GAZPACHO

*When Georgie and Cyndi moved to Greeley in the '70s, they belonged to a newcomers recipe group. This soup was especially popular when gardens were producing fresh veggies.*

1 large tomato, peeled
1 clove garlic, washed and peeled
1 large cucumber, pared, cut in pieces
1 medium onion, cut in pieces
1 green pepper, cleaned and cut in pieces
1 46-ounce can tomato juice
1/4 cup olive oil
1/3 cup wine vinegar
1/4 teaspoon liquid hot pepper
1 1/2 teaspoon salt
1/4 teaspoon coarse black pepper
1 cup croutons
1/4 cup chives, chopped

In blender, combine 1/2 of tomato, cucumber, onion, green pepper and tomato juice. Add garlic. Blend until smooth. In large bowl or pitcher, combine pureed vegetables and remaining tomato juice, olive oil, vinegar and seasonings. Chill at least 2 hours. Coarsely chop remaining vegetables, one at a time, and place in small bowls to pass as garnish. Ladle soup into chilled bowls; garnish with croutons and chives. Serve as a luncheon starter or entree accompanied by salad and bread. Serves 12.

*Per serving: 78 calories; 4.8 fat grams*

 Chopped vegetables can be added to the soup before serving.

# MUSHROOM BISQUE

2 teaspoons olive oil
1 cup fresh shiitake mushrooms, sliced,
    stems removed
1 cup fresh oyster mushrooms
1 large onion, chopped
1 clove garlic, chopped
1 12-ounce can evaporated skim milk
1 14-ounce can low sodium chicken broth
1 teaspoon thyme
1 teaspoon seasoned pepper
2 tablespoons flour
1/3 cup light sour cream
2 tablespoons parsley

In large saucepan, combine oil, mushrooms, onion and garlic; saute 5 minutes. Place mushroom mixture in blender or food processor. Cover and whirl until smooth. Return to sauce pan. Stir in milk, broth, thyme and pepper. Heat to boiling; reduce heat. Cover and simmer 5 minutes. Stir flour into sour cream. Gradually stir 1 cup hot soup into sour cream mixture. Return to soup mixture; cook, stirring constantly until thickened. Ladle into bowls. Sprinkle with parsley. Serves 4.

*Per serving: 220 calories; 10.6 fat grams*

# HOMEMADE TOMATO SOUP

*This is a very easy, QUICK soup to prepare. It's low in fat, cholesterol and calories with a wonderful fresh flavor.*

2 cups tomato juice (or use 8 fresh tomatoes, skinned and pureed in blender)
3 cups skim milk
3 tablespoons cornstarch
3/4 teaspoon basil

In large pan, stir all ingredients together. Heat to boiling, reduce heat, stirring constantly. Continue to simmer, stirring, until thickened. Dilute with a bit of water if too thick. Serves 4.

*Per serving: 116 calories; 0.4 fat grams*

Our favorite way to serve tomato soup is with grilled cheese sandwiches NOT low in fat. Try combining swiss, colby and white cheddar on wholegrained bread, and pan grill until lightly browned on both buttered sides.

# TOMATO CABBAGE SOUP

1 19-ounce can crushed tomatoes
2 cups cabbage, grated, packed
1/2 cup onion, chopped
2 beef bouillon cubes
2 cups boiling water
1/2 teaspoon sugar
1/4 cup fresh or frozen peas, optional

In medium pan, combine tomatoes, cabbage and onion. Dissolve bouillon in boiling water. Add to tomato mixture. Bring to boil. Cover and simmer on low heat 20 minutes. Add sugar and peas. Simmer 5 minutes. Ladle into soup bowls. Serves 4.

*Per serving: 50 calories; 0.5 fat grams*

 Studies show that eating cabbage reduces the risk of developing colon cancer.

# TOMATO SOUP WITH AVOCADO

*Too easy to be true.*

1 10-ounce can condensed tomato soup
1 soup can water
1 14-ounce can beef broth
1/4 teaspoon oregano
1/8 teaspoon garlic powder
1 avocado, thinly sliced

Combine soup, water, beef broth, oregano and garlic powder. Heat to boiling, reduce heat and simmer 5 minutes, stirring occasionally. Pour into bowls. Float thin slices of avocado on each bowl of soup. Serves 4.

*Per serving: 139 calories; 7.8 fat grams*

 Serve this tasty soup with slices of toasted French bread with cheese broiled on top.

# EASY TOMATO VEGETABLE SOUP

1 10-ounce can condensed tomato soup
1 soup cans water
1/2 teaspoon lemon juice
1/8 teaspoon ground nutmeg
1/2 16-ounce package frozen seasoned
    pasta with vegetables

In large saucepan, combine soup and water. Add lemon juice, nutmeg and vegetables. Heat to boiling, reduce heat and simmer 15 minutes. Serves 4.

*Per serving: 91 calories; 2.2 fat grams*

Try different types of packaged pasta with vegetables. Or, increase water to 1 1/2 soup cans and use 1 10-ounce can condensed vegetable soup.

# VEGETABLE SOUP

*Use fresh garden vegetables to enhance that robust vegetable flavor.*

3-4 potatoes, diced
1 large onion, finely chopped
1/2 cup carrots, finely chopped
5 cups zucchini, finely chopped
1/2 cup celery, chopped
1 cup peas, fresh or frozen
6 cups water
2 chicken bouillon cubes
1 teaspoon lemon juice
3/4 teaspoon tarragon
1/2 teaspoon parsley flakes
Salt and pepper to taste
Low-fat yogurt or sour cream, optional

In large pan, combine all ingredients except salt, pepper and yogurt. Bring to boil, lower heat and cover. Simmer 20 minutes. Add salt and pepper. Simmer 5 minutes. Ladle into soup bowls and top with dollop of yogurt or sour cream. Serves 6-8.

*Per serving: 86 calories; 0.4 fat grams*

For QUICK preparation and smoother soup, chop vegetables, except peas, in blender or food processor. This will make a thicker soup without adding calories.

# MEATLESS MINESTRONE

2 tablespoons olive oil
2 tablespoons corn oil
1 onion, chopped
2 cloves garlic, chopped
2 stalks celery, diced
2 carrots, diced
2 potatoes, peeled and cubed
1 small zucchini, diced
1 15-ounce can chopped tomatoes
1 8-ounce can green beans
8 cups water
1 15-ounce can Great Northern beans
1/2 cup leftover cooked rice or pasta
1 tablespoon basil
1/2 cup parmesan cheese

In large pan, combine onion, garlic, celery, carrots and oils. Saute 10 minutes, stirring occasionally. Add potatoes, zucchini, tomatoes, green beans and water. Bring to boil; reduce heat and simmer 30 minutes. Add beans, pasta and basil. Ladle into soup bowls. Garnish with parmesan cheese. Serves 8.

*Per serving: 264 calories; 9.0 fat grams*

# CREAM OF ZUCCHINI SOUP

*For those of us who grow zucchini, and for those we give it to, we are always looking for ways to use it.*

3 cups zucchini, sliced
1/2 cup water
1/4 cup onion, finely chopped
1 teaspoon mixed seasoning spices
1/2 teaspoon parsley
1 tablespoon chicken bouillon granules
2 tablespoons butter
2 tablespoons flour
1/8 teaspoon white pepper
1/4 teaspoon celery seed
1 cup milk
1/2 cup light cream
4 tablespoons light sour cream
Paprika
Slivered almonds

In medium pan, combine first 5 ingredients and 1 teaspoon bouillon. Cook 10 minutes, only a small amount of water should be left. Pour into blender or food processor and whirl until smooth. In small saucepan, combine butter, flour, remaining bouillon, water and seasonings. Blend well. Add milk and cream; simmer until thickened, stirring constantly. Add zucchini mixture and stir well. Add more milk, if too thick. Serve topped with dollop of sour cream; sprinkle generously with paprika and slivered almonds. Serves 5-6.

*Per serving: 189 calories; 15.0 fat grams*

# HOT AND SOUR SOUP

*A traditional soup served at Chinese restaurants; easy to make at home. Substitute with different vegetables and meats . . . or no meat at all.*

1/4 pound lean pork, cut into matchstick
    pieces
2 15-ounce cans chicken broth
1 boneless chicken breast, skinned, cut into
    matchstick pieces
1 4-ounce can mushrooms, sliced, drained
1/2 cup bamboo shoots, cut in matchstick
    pieces
1/4 pound bean curd or tofu, drained and
    cut in 1/2-inch cubes
2 tablespoons white wine vinegar
1 tablespoon soy sauce
2 tablespoons cornstarch
1/4 cup water
3/4 teaspoon white pepper
1 teaspoon sesame oil
1 egg, lightly beaten
2 whole green onions, cut diagonally in
    1-inch pieces
1/4-1/2 teaspoon salt, optional

In large pan, bring broth to boiling. Add pork, chicken broth, chicken, mushrooms and bamboo shoots. Stir several times, then reduce heat; cover and simmer 5 minutes. Add bean curd, vinegar and soy. Heat 1 minute. In small bowl, blend cornstarch and water. Add to soup and simmer, stirring, until slightly thickened. Turn off heat. Add pepper and sesame oil. Stirring constantly, slowly pour egg into soup. Add onion and salt to taste. Serves 6.

*Per serving: 309 calories; 16.2 fat grams*

# MINESTRONE SOUP

*Cyndi's dear friend, Nursey Bev, shared this recipe using a soup mix. It takes a little more time to prepare, but worth the effort. Remember, the beans need to be soaked 8 hours.*

1 6-ounce package minestrone soup mix (complete mix found in the bean/lentil section of store), presoaked 8 hours
5 cups water
1 pound lean ground beef, cubed pork or cubed beef
1 medium onion, chopped
1 clove garlic, minced
1 carrot, sliced
1 stalk celery, sliced
1 16-ounce can Italian plum tomatoes
1/2 teaspoon marjoram
1/2 teaspoon basil
1/4 teaspoon oregano
1 bay leaf
Salt and pepper to taste
1/3 cup uncooked elbow macaroni or broken spaghetti
Parmesan cheese

In large pan, bring soup mix and water to boil. Reduce heat. Brown meat with onion and garlic; add to bean mixture. Add carrot, celery, tomatoes and spices. Cover and simmer 45 minutes. Add more liquid, if needed. Add macaroni or spaghetti and simmer another 10 minutes. Ladle into soup bowls and top with parmesan cheese. Serve with bread and salad. Serves 6-8.

*Per serving: 309 calories; 16.2 fat grams*

This a great soup for the slow cooker. Brown ground beef and put in slow cooker with all ingredients except macaroni. Cook on low 10-11 hours. Add macaroni 1 hour before serving.

# MEXICAN VEGETABLE SOUP

*Use leftover taco meat and plain or seasoned rice in this recipe. Or, be creative and use leftover fajita meat and vegetables. This is a good soup for improvising with meat and vegetables.*

2 beef bouillon cubes
2 cups water
2 15-ounce cans beef broth
1/2 teaspoon taco seasoning
1 teaspoon hot pepper sauce
1 teaspoon garlic powder
1 teaspoon cumin
1 teaspoon salt
3 carrots, diced
1 celery stalk, diced
1/2 onion, chopped
2 small zucchinis, diced
3/4 cup cauliflower, diced
1 1/2 cups taco seasoned cooked ground
    beef
1 cup rice, cooked

In large pan, combine broth and seasonings. Bring to boil; simmer 10 minutes. Add vegetables, meat and rice to broth. Simmer 30 minutes. Serves 8-10.

*Per serving: 181 calories; 9.1 fat grams*

# TACO SOUP

1 pound lean ground beef, browned and
    drained
2 16-ounce cans chicken broth
1 14-ounce can mexicorn
2 cups mild salsa
1 16-ounce black beans
3/4 cup tortilla chips
1/2 cup cheddar cheese, shredded

Combine all ingredients, except chips and cheese. Over medium heat, simmer 10 minutes. Ladle soup into bowls; top with chips and cheese. Serves 6-8.

*Per serving: 548 calories; 29.6 fat grams*

 Substitute cooked, diced chicken for beef if fewer calories are desired.

# QUICK BEEF AND NOODLE SOUP

*A good recipe to use leftover beef roast, steak, hamburger, pork or chicken.*

2 cups leftover beef roast, julienned
1 16-ounce can beef broth
1 can water
3 medium carrots, sliced
2 medium onions, chopped
2 stalks celery, diced
1 6-ounce can sliced mushrooms, optional
1 12-ounce package egg noodles, cooked
    and drained
1/2 teaspoon salt
2 tablespoons soy sauce
1 tablespoon catsup
1 1/2 teaspoons cornstarch

In large pan, combine beef, beef broth, water, carrots, onions, celery and mushrooms. Bring to boil and simmer 15 minutes. Add noodles and salt. Continue to simmer. In small bowl, mix together soy sauce, catsup and cornstarch. Slowly add to beef mixture, stirring until thickened. Simmer 10 minutes. Serves 4.

*Per serving: 354 calories; 14.9 fat grams*

 Foot Note | When using chicken or pork, substitute chicken broth for beef broth.

# BACON CHEESEBURGER SOUP

1 pound lean ground beef
1 onion, chopped
1 clove garlic, minced
2 carrots, diced
1/4 cup green pepper, diced
2 tablespoons diced jalapeño pepper
2 boiled potatoes, peeled and diced
1 tablespoon beef bouillon granules
1/2 teaspoon cayenne pepper
11/2 cups water
2 1/2 cups milk
1 1/2 cup process American cheese, cubed
1/2 pound sliced bacon, cooked and crumbled

In large pan, brown ground beef; drain. Add onion, garlic, carrots, green pepper and jalapeño. Cover and simmer 10 minutes, stirring occasionally. Stir in potatoes, bouillon, cayenne, water and milk. Stir and bring to boil. Simmer 5 minutes. Add cheese and stir until melted. Ladle into soup bowls and top with bacon. Serves 6-8.

*Per serving: 540 calories; 40.1 fat grams*

 If using raw potatoes, dice and add with other vegetables and increase cooking time 10 minutes.

# OLD FASHIONED CHILI

*Gotta love it on the first day it snows.*

2 pounds lean ground beef
1 onion, chopped
2 cloves garlic, diced
1/2 cup celery, diced
4 cups tomato juice
1 15-ounce can tomato puree
1 15-ounce can kidney beans, drained
1 15-ounce can small red beans, drained
1 15-ounce can water
1/4 cup chili powder
2 teaspoons cumin
1 teaspoon garlic powder
1/2 teaspoon salt
1 teaspoon pepper
1 teaspoon oregano
1 teaspoon sugar
1/2 teaspoon cayenne pepper

In large pan, brown beef; drain. Add onion, garlic and celery. Cook 5 minutes. Add remaining ingredients. Cover and simmer 45 minutes, stirring occasionally. Serve with chopped onions and shredded cheese on top. Serves 12-16.

*Per serving: 423 calories; 14.5 fat grams*

 If you prefer, substitute 2 15-ounce cans pinto beans in chili gravy for the red beans.

# BREW PUB CHILI

*It has a lot of ingredients, but is easy to assemble for your quick cold-day meal.*

2 1/2 pounds lean ground beef or turkey
1 large onion, chopped
3 cloves garlic, minced
2 stalks celery, sliced
1 green pepper, chopped
1 2-ounce jar pimentos
1 16-ounce can kidney beans
1 16-ounce can tomatoes, cut up
1 teaspoon cumin
1 teaspoon pepper
2 teaspoons celery salt
2 tablespoons chili powder
Dash cayenne pepper
1 tablespoon brown sugar
1 6-ounce can tomato paste
1 cup water
2 tablespoons Worcestershire sauce
2 tablespoons barbecue sauce
1 tablespoon soy sauce

In large pan, cook meat and drain. Add remaining ingredients and mix. Simmer for 30-45 minutes. If too thick, add another can of tomatoes or a cup of water. Serve with cheese, onions, crackers, tortillas or over a baked potato. Serves 8.

*Per serving: 623 calories; 30.7 fat grams*

 Serve in a bread bowl for a conversation piece dinner.

# GROUND BEEF VEGETABLE SOUP

1/2 pound lean ground beef
1/2 cup onion, chopped
1/2 cup celery, chopped
1 16-ounce can cut-up tomatoes
3 medium potatoes, diced
1 8-ounce can green beans
1 teaspoon chili powder
1/2 teaspoon salt
1/2 teaspoon Worcestershire sauce
Dash cayenne
1 10-ounce can condensed beef broth
1 soup can water

In large pan, cook ground beef; drain. Add onion and celery; cook 5 minutes. Add remaining ingredients. Bring to boil; reduce heat and simmer 45 minutes. Serves 6.

*Per serving: 179 calories; 8.7 fat grams*

# VEGETABLE BEEF STEW

*Turnips are Georgie's favorite addition to stews. They add a unique flavor and texture to any vegetable soup.*

2 cups leftover, cooked roast beef
1 15-ounce can crushed tomatoes
1 10-ounce can condensed tomato soup
1 onion, chopped
3 cups water
2 bay leaves
1 tablespoon salt
2 teaspoons Worcestershire sauce
1/4 teaspoon chili powder
1 16-ounce package frozen mixed soup
    vegetables
1 turnip, coarsely diced
2 potatoes, coarsely diced
1 cup celery, diced

In large pan, combine all ingredients. Bring to boil; reduce heat and simmer 45 minutes (if using slow cooker, cook 4-6 hours). Serve with biscuits or corn bread. Serves 12.

*Per serving: 272 calories; 7.1 fat grams*

# SOUTHWESTERN BEEF STEW

*Big chunks of fresh vegetables and salsa makes this a spicy crowd pleaser.*

2 pounds boneless, lean beef stew meat, cut
    in 1-inch pieces
2 tablespoons flour
2 tablespoons oil
1 10-ounce can condensed beef broth
1 cup hot water
1 cup salsa
1 medium onion, coarsely chopped
1/4 cup parsley
1 teaspoon salt
1 teaspoon cumin
2 cloves garlic, minced
1 15-ounce can Mexican tomatoes
1 16-ounce package frozen soup mix
    vegetables
1 small zucchini, sliced
2 ears fresh or thawed frozen corn, cut in
    1-inch pieces

In large pan, combine meat and flour; brown in oil on medium heat 10 minutes. Add remaining ingredients and simmer 40 minutes. If thicker stew is preferred, mix 1-2 tablespoons flour with 1/2 cup water and gradually add to simmering stew, stirring until slightly thickened. Ladle into soup bowls or individual bread bowls. Serves 8.

*Per serving: 370 calories; 11.9 fat grams*

# EASY CREAM OF CHICKEN VEGETABLE SOUP

1 cup celery, minced
1/2 cup carrot, minced
1/2 cup onion, minced
2 cups water
1 10-ounce can cream of chicken soup
1 10-ounce can cream of celery soup
1 cup milk

In large pan, combine vegetables and water. Cook on medium heat, stirring occasionally, 15 minutes. Drain, reserving 1 cup liquid. Combine reserved vegetable liquid, canned soups and milk with vegetables. Heat to serving temperature and ladle into soup bowls. Serves 4.

*Per serving: 109 calories; 5.9 fat grams*

 Add leftover cooked meat and vegetables to this soup to make it heartier.

# CHICKEN-MUSHROOM SOUP

2 chicken breasts, cooked and diced
2 1/3 cups water
1 bay leaf
1/2 teaspoon salt
1/4 teaspoon pepper
1/2 cup onion, chopped
1 cup mushrooms, sliced
1 10-ounce can condensed cream of chicken soup
1 cup carrots, grated
1 cup peas, fresh or frozen

Combine chicken, water, bay leaf, salt and pepper in medium saucepan. Bring to boil and simmer 15 minutes. Discard bay leaf. Add onion, mushrooms, soup and carrots. Cover and simmer 20-30 minutes until vegetables are tender. Add peas and simmer 5 minutes. Ladle into soup bowls and serve with biscuits or crusty bread. Serves 6.

*Per serving: 159 calories; 3.9 fat grams*

 This is a great soup to use up leftover chicken or turkey.

# CHICKEN BARLEY CHILI

*A hearty, easy to prepare chili to take the chill off after a hard day of playing in the snow.*

1 cup onion, chopped
1 clove garlic, chopped
1 tablespoon oil
2 cups water
3/4 cup quick barley
1 15-ounce can crushed tomatoes
1 15-ounce can tomato sauce
1 14-ounce can low sodium chicken broth
1 11-ounce can corn, drained
1 4-ounce can chopped green chilies
2 tablespoons chili powder
1 teaspoon cumin
1/2 teaspoon oregano
3 cups cooked chicken, chopped

In large pan, cook onion and garlic in oil 5 minutes. Add remaining ingredients, except chicken. Bring to boil. Reduce heat, cover and simmer 10 minutes, stirring occasionally. Add chicken and simmer 10 minutes. Add additional water or chicken broth if chili is too thick. Serves 8-10.

*Per serving: 197 calories; 3.8 fat grams*

Barley is a healthy substitute for pasta or rice in other soups. Barley is cholesterol and sodium free; it is low in fat and a good source of fiber.

## VEGETABLE CHICKEN NOODLE SOUP

*We like this soup thinner in consistency so we can enjoy a freshly baked biscuit on top to absorb the broth.*

2 tablespoons butter
1 onion, chopped
1 clove garlic, chopped
2 stalks celery, sliced
2 carrots, diced
1/2 cup frozen peas, thawed
1/2 cup okra, optional
4 chicken bouillon cubes
8 cups water
2 bay leaves
1/2 teaspoon thyme
1 teaspoon parsley
2 cups cooked chicken, diced
2 cups cooked noodles

In large pan, combine butter, onion and garlic; saute 5 minutes. Add remaining ingredients, except noodles, and simmer 30 minutes. Add noodles and simmer 10 minutes. Serves 8.

*Per serving: 170 calories; 7.9 fat grams*

Foot Note

If a thicker soup is desired, combine 3 tablespoons cornstarch with 1/4 cup water and pour into soup mixture, stirring until thick.

# CHICKEN CHILE SOUP

*This is a favorite from our Quick Crockery Cooking cookbook, unanimously requested to be included in this cookbook.*

4 chicken breast halves, cooked and shredded (for trade shows and quick preparation, we use 2 10-ounce cans white chunk chicken)

2 16-ounce cans chicken broth

1 teaspoon lemon pepper

1 clove garlic, minced

1 cup onion, chopped

2 9-ounce packages frozen white corn, thawed

2 4-ounce cans green chilies

1 1/2 teaspoons cumin

2-3 tablespoons lime juice

1 15-ounce cans Great Northern white beans, undrained

2/3 cup baked tortilla chips, crushed, optional

2/3 cup Monterey Jack cheese (can use reduced-fat, if desired), optional

In large pan, combine all ingredients, except tortilla chips and cheese. Bring to boiling; reduce heat and simmer 30 minutes. Ladle into soup bowls. Top with tortilla chips and cheese. Serves 8.

*Per serving: 589 calories; 10.4 fat grams*

This soup can be prepared in the microwave. Cook the chicken in a microwavable bowl or pan. And, of course, it's a great soup for the slow cooker.

# CAMPERS' QUICK HAM CHOWDER

*You won't need to be in the kitchen long with this recipe.*

1 1/2 cups cooked ham, diced
1 10-ounce can cream of mushroom soup
1 15-ounce can sliced potatoes, drained
1 8-ounce can sliced carrots, drained
1 8-ounce can cut green beans, drained
1 1/2 cups water or milk

In medium pan, combine ham, soup and vegetables. Stir in water or milk. Bring to boil; reduce heat. Simmer 5 minutes. Ladle into bowls. Serve with biscuits, bread or crackers. Serves 4-6.

*Per serving: 207 calories; 6.9 fat grams*

Try different soups, meats and vegetables when making this soup. How about using the franks that were left from the campfire roasting the night before?

# SOUTHERN TURKEY MEATBALL SOUP

*This hearty soup is easy and colorful.*

3/4 pound ground turkey
1/3 cup tortilla chips, finely crushed
2/3 cup salsa
1/2 teaspoon salt
1 onion, chopped
1 clove garlic, minced
2 tablespoons oil
3/4 teaspoon cumin
2 15-ounce cans chicken broth
1 cup water
1/2 cup uncooked rice
1 cup frozen corn, thawed, or 1 8-ounce
    can corn
1 16-ounce can kidney beans, drained

In medium bowl, combine turkey, tortilla chips, 1/3 cup salsa and salt. Form into 1 inch balls. In large pan, combine onion, garlic and oil; cook 3 minutes. Add remaining salsa, cumin, broth and water. Bring to boil. Add rice and meatballs. Cover and simmer 15 minutes. Add corn and beans; simmer 5 minutes. Ladle into soup bowls and serve with cornbread. Serves 8.

*Per serving: 252 calories; 11.7 fat grams*

 To save time, form meatballs while salsa mixture is coming to a boil. Drop them in as they are made.

# TURKEY TORTILLA SOUP

1 tablespoon oil or butter
1 cup onion, chopped
2 cups cooked turkey, diced
1 4-ounce can green chiles, chopped
1 package taco seasoning mix
1 16-ounce can tomatoes, cut up
6 cups turkey stock or bouillon
2 cups frozen corn
1/3 cup fresh cilantro, chopped
1/2 cup tortilla chips, broken
3/4 cup Monterey Jack cheese, shredded

In large pan, saute onion in oil. Add all ingredients except tortilla chips and cheese. Simmer for 30 minutes. Ladle into bowls and top with chips and cheese. Serves 6-8.

*Per serving: 331 calories; 14.3 fat grams*

 In some grocery and gourmet stores, you can find bags of colored tortilla strips. They make a colorful alternative to regular tortilla chips.

# CAMPFIRE STEW

*The smoky flavor brings a touch of outdoor adventure to the dinner table.*

1/2 pound Polish sausage, cut into 1/4-inch
    slices
2 15-ounce cans pinto beans (do not drain)
2 onions, chopped
1 cup tomato juice
1/2 cup salsa
1 medium green pepper, coarsely chopped
1 teaspoon chili powder
1/2 teaspoon cumin
1/2 teaspoon oregano
1/4 cup fresh cilantro, chopped

Combine all ingredients, except cilantro; bring to boil. Cover and simmer 20 minutes. Ladle into soup bowls; top with cilantro. Serves 6.

*Per serving: 266 calories; 12.3 fat grams*

# QUICK CLAM CHOWDER

*The story behind this recipe goes like this: A friend Zona was ushering company out of the front door one hour before expecting guests for dinner. By the time, guests arrived, she had prepared this soup on top of stove (usually all done in the microwave), set a beautiful table, picked up from the last group of guests and was calmly poised to serve a lovely dinner with salad, bread and dessert. The soup was 'gourmetishly' delicious making us think she had worked on it all day.*

3 slices bacon, diced
1/4 cup onion, diced
1/4 cup celery, diced
1/4 cup green pepper
1 15-ounce can clam chowder
1 3/4 cup half and half
1 tablespoon butter
1/4 teaspoon celery salt
1/4 teaspoon thyme
Salt and pepper to taste
1/4 cup white wine
Parsley
Paprika

In large microwavable bowl, combine bacon, onion, celery and green pepper; cook at high setting 4-5 minutes stirring twice. Drain. Add remaining ingredients, except wine; microwave at 50% setting 15 minutes, stirring twice. Add wine and heat on high 1 minute. Ladle into soup bowls. Garnish with parsley and paprika. Serves 4.

*Per serving: 285 calories; 21.9 fat grams*

# CLAM CHOWDER

*A nutritious, lowfat chowder.*

2 medium potatoes, diced finely
1/2 cup carrot, grated
1 medium onion, finely chopped
1 stalk celery, finely chopped
2 cups water
2 tablespoons flour
1/2 teaspoon salt
1/8 teaspoon pepper
1 cup low fat milk
1 tablespoon butter, optional
1 5-ounce can chopped clams with juice

In large pan, cook potato, carrot, onion and celery in water 15 minutes until vegetables are tender. With potato masher, mash about 1/2 of vegetables in pot. In small bowl, mix flour, salt and pepper in milk until smooth. Stir into boiling soup until thickened, stirring constantly. Add butter and stir until melted. Add clams with juice, and heat through. Ladle into soup bowls and serve with crunchy salad and favorite bread. Serves 4.

*Per serving: 111 calories; 3.6 fat grams*

# CRAB AND CORN CHOWDER

*It is easy, delicious and NOT low in fat or calories. Use leftover baked potatoes or parsley potatoes to make this recipe quicker.*

1 tablespoons oil
1 small onion, diced
1 stalk celery, diced
1/2 pound lump crab meat
1 8-ounce bottle clam juice
2 baked potatoes, peeled and diced
1 8-ounce can corn, drained
2 15-ounce cans chicken broth
1 tablespoon Worcestershire sauce
1 1/2 teaspoon hot pepper sauce
3/4 teaspoon thyme
1/4 teaspoon white pepper
1 12-ounce can evaporated milk or 1/2 cup
    cream
3 tablespoons butter
3 tablespoons flour

In large pan, combine oil, onion and celery; saute 3 minutes. Add all other ingredients, except thyme, white pepper, cream, butter and flour. Simmer 30 minutes. Add thyme, pepper and cream. In small skillet, melt butter. Stir in flour. Bring soup to boil, but do not boil. Add the flour and butter mixture, stirring constantly. Soup will thicken. Remove and serve in soup bowls. Serves 4-6.

*Per serving: 401 calories; 17.5 fat grams*

If butter and flour mixture is lumpy or stiff, stir in 1 cup of the hot soup until smooth. Slowly add mixture to soup, stirring constantly.

# SEAFOOD CHOWDER BY COMMITTEE

*Have each guest bring a main ingredient for this soup. You take care of onion, celery, carrot, butter and seasonings. This committee idea works well for most soup or salad recipes.*

1 onion, chopped
2 stalks celery, chopped
1 carrot, chopped
1 tablespoon butter
4 cups half and half
1 10-ounce can condensed clam chowder
1 8-ounce bottle clam juice
3 potatoes, peeled and cubed
1 10-ounce can corn, drained
1 teaspoon salt
1/4 teaspoon white pepper
1 8-ounce package imitation crabmeat,
    flaked
1 pound shrimp, cooked and shelled
8 small bread bowls

In large pan, saute onion, celery and carrot with butter 3-4 minutes. Add remaining ingredients, except bread. Bring to a boil; reduce heat and simmer 20 minutes. Ladle into bread bowls. Serves 8.

*Per serving: 433 calories; 18.2 fat grams*

# CRAB BISQUE

1 10-ounce can condensed cream of mushroom soup
1 10-ounce can condensed cream of asparagus soup
1 1/2 soup cans lowfat milk
1 cup light cream
1 cup crab meat
1/4 cup cooking sherry
2 tablespoons butter

In large pan, blend soups; stir in milk and cream. Heat just to boiling. Add crab meat; heat through. Do not boil. Add cooking sherry just before serving. Ladle into soup bowls; float 1/2 teaspoon butter on top of each. Serves 6-8.

*Per serving: 118 calories; 6.0 fat grams*

# CRAB PASTA CHOWDER

*This delicious soup is our attempt to duplicate one served by a popular restaurant in Colorado.*

6 ounces miniature bow tie pasta or shells, cooked
3 tablespoons butter
1 cup fresh mushrooms, sliced
1 16-ounce jar Alfredo sauce
2 cups milk
1 1/2 cups water
1/4 cup dry white wine or 2 tablespoons white wine vinegar
1/4 cup green onions, sliced
3 ounces crab meat, frozen or canned
Parsley for garnish

In medium pan, melt butter. Add mushrooms and saute 3 minutes. Add sauce, milk, water and wine. Stir well with wire whip over moderate heat until mixture comes to boil. Reduce heat and simmer 5-8 minutes, stirring constantly. Add green onions, pasta and crab meat; stir. Ladle into soup bowls. Sprinkle with parsley. Serve immediately. Serves 6.

*Per serving: 295 calories; 10.6 fat grams*

# SHRIMP NEWBURG SOUP

2 10-ounce cans condensed cream of
   shrimp soup
2 cups lowfat milk
2 cups medium cooked shrimp
3/4 cup frozen peas
1/4 cup sherry, optional
1 cup sharp cheddar cheese, shredded

In large pan, combine all ingredients except sherry and cheese. Heat over medium heat, stirring often, just to simmering point. Reduce heat and cook 5 minutes. Stir in sherry and half of cheese. To serve, spoon soup into bowls and top with remaining cheese. Serves 8.

*Per serving: 477 calories; 22.2 fat grams*

 For a shrimp Newburg entree, reduce milk to 1/2 cup. Serve over biscuits or patty shells and sprinkle with remaining cheese.

# PASTA SOUP

*This is a thick soup that was created by Cyndi when camping in Australia to use what was in the refrigerator.*

2-3 tablespoons light margarine
1 carrot, diced
1 medium leek, sliced (white portion only)
1/4 cup green pepper, diced
2 cloves garlic, minced
1/2 cup spiral pasta
1 1/2 cups mushrooms, sliced
1 cup water
1/2 16-ounce jar mushroom/garlic pasta
    sauce
1/2-3/4 cup lowfat milk
Salt and pepper to taste

In large saucepan, melt margarine; add carrot, onion, green pepper and garlic. Saute 3-4 minutes. Add pasta, mushrooms and water. Simmer 15 minutes. Add pasta sauce and milk. Add more milk for a thinner soup. Heat to boiling; lower heat. Season with salt and pepper. Ladle into soup bowls and serve with salad and bread. Serves 4.

*Per serving: 144 calories; 6.1 fat grams*

Substitute 1/2 cup white wine for part of the milk.

If you prefer, substitute your favorite tomato based pasta sauce.

# SPICY MACARONI SOUP

1 pound lean ground beef
1 medium onion, chopped
5 cups water
1 15-ounce can pinto beans, rinsed and
    drained
1 15-ounce can diced tomatoes, undrained
1 7-ounce can corn, drained
1 4-ounce can chopped green chiles
1/2 teaspoon brown mustard
1/2 teaspoon salt
1/8 teaspoon pepper
1 7-ounce package macaroni and cheese,
    reserving the cheese packet
1 1.5-ounce packet taco seasoning mix
1/2 cup shredded Monterey Jack cheese

In large pan, brown beef; drain. Stir in onion and cook 2-3 minutes. Add remaining ingredients except cheese and taco seasoning. Bring to boil. Reduce heat; cover and simmer 15 minutes. Stir in cheese and seasoning mixes. Cover and simmer 10 minutes. Ladle into soup bowls and top with teaspoon of cheese. Serves 8-10.

*Per serving: 451 calories; 14.6 fat grams*

# MELON SOUP

*A delicious chilled soup to start a meal.*

3 cups cantaloupe, diced
3 cups honeydew melon, diced
2 cups orange juice
1/3 cup lime juice
4 tablespoons honey
2 cups gingerale, dry champagne or white
    wine
Whipped topping
Mint leaves

Reserve half of diced fruit. In blender or food processor, puree remaining half of fruit with juices and honey. Pour into large bowl. Stir in gingerale and reserve fruit. Cover and refrigerate. Serve in chilled bowls; garnish with whipped topping and mint leaves.

*Per serving: 209 calories; 0.5 fat grams*

# FRESH PEACH SOUP

3 cups fresh peaches, peeled and sliced
1/4 cup apricot nectar
1/8 teaspoon nutmeg
1 8-ounce carton lite vanilla yogurt
Nutmeg, optional
Fresh raspberries for garnish

In blender or food processor, puree all ingredients except nutmeg and raspberries until smooth. Cover and chill. Serve as a starter in dessert or wine glasses. Garnish with nutmeg and two or three raspberries. Serves 4.

*Per serving: 99 calories; 0.8 fat grams*

Raspberries help prevent heart disease because they have a natural form of aspirin.

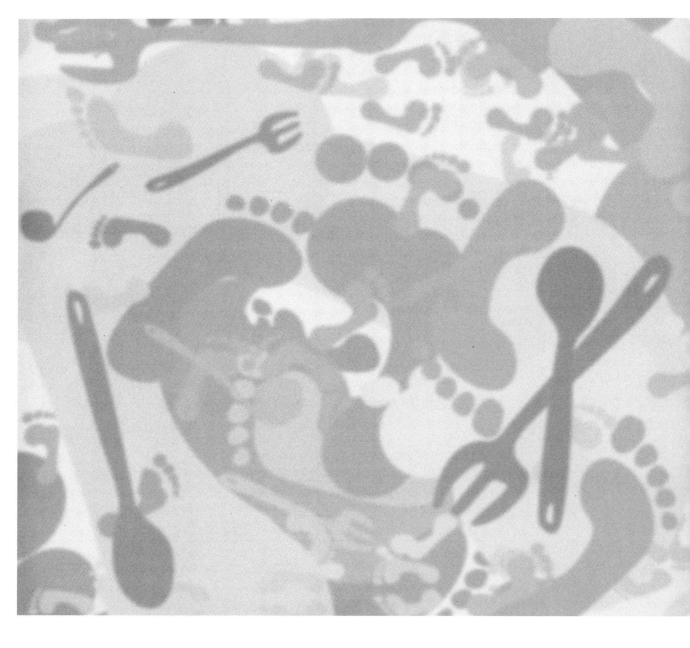

# Salads

# ARTICHOKE SALAD

*Great to serve when entertaining.*

1/2 cup oil
1/3 cup vinegar
2 tablespoons water
4 thin slices onion
1 tablespoon sugar
1 clove garlic, crushed
1/2 teaspoon salt
1/4 teaspoon celery seed
Dash pepper
1 14-ounce can artichoke hearts
4 cups Bibb lettuce
8 cherry tomatoes, halved

In container with lid, combine oil, vinegar, water, onion, sugar, garlic, salt, celery seed and pepper. Cover and shake well. Add artichoke hearts, refrigerate and allow to marinate until ready to serve. At serving time, drain artichokes, reserving dressing. Toss artichokes with lettuce and tomatoes. Add enough reserved dressing to coat lettuce. Toss again. Serves 6.

*Per serving: 248 calories; 15.1 fat grams*

 Save leftover dressing to use on other tossed salads.

# ARTICHOKE-CREAM CHEESE TOSS

1/2 head Romaine lettuce, torn
1/2 head iceberg lettuce, torn
1/2 cup fresh mushrooms, sliced
1 14-ounce can water-packed artichoke
    hearts, drained and rinsed
2 ounces cream cheese, cut into small
    chunks
3-5 green onions, chopped


Dressing
1 cup oil
1/4 cup red wine vinegar
1/3 cup sugar
1 tablespoon celery seed
1 teaspoon dry mustard
1 teaspoon salt
1/4 cup onion, minced
Dash pepper

Combine all ingredients in large bowl and toss with dressing.  Serves 6-8.


Dressing
Combine in covered container and shake to blend. Pour over salad.


*Per serving: 392 calories; 34.6 fat grams*

# ASPARAGUS SALAD

*This is a delicious and easy springtime recipe.*

1/2 cup light Italian dressing
1 pound asparagus spears, cooked
12 red onion rings
Bibb or Boston lettuce leaves
2 hard-boiled eggs, sieved

Pour dressing over asparagus and onions. Cover and marinate in refrigerator several hours or overnight. Drain, reserving marinade. Arrange on lettuce-covered salad plates. Top with eggs. Serve marinade on the side. Serves 4.

*Per serving: 213 calories; 16.7 fat grams*

For quick and easy preparation, microwave asparagus on high about 4 minutes with 2 tablespoons water. Be sure to trim tough portion of stalk.

# ASPARAGUS-TOMATO DUO

3 slices bacon, cooked crisp, cooled and
    crumbled
1/4 cup green onions, sliced
1/4 cup oil
3 tablespoons red wine vinegar
1 tablespoon water
2 teaspoons sugar
1/4 teaspoon salt
1 1/2 pounds fresh asparagus, bias-cut
2 medium tomatoes, cut in wedges

In medium pan, combine bacon, onion, oil, vinegar, water, sugar and salt. Bring to boil. Add asparagus. Cover and cook 5 minutes. Drain and reserve liquid; chill. Add tomato wedges to asparagus; chill until ready to serve. On 6 salad plates, arrange asparagus and tomatoes on top of lettuce leaf. Pour reserved liquid over salad. Serves 6.

*Per serving: 207 calories; 9.9 fat grams*

Always cook extra bacon, crumble and freeze to use for special recipes or as a garnish.

# BEET SALAD

*This salad is one of Georgie's mom's favorites and a great addition to a tossed salad. It is an easy recipe to double.*

1 16-ounce can sliced beets
2 tablespoons sugar
1 tablespoon vinegar
1 small onion, sliced into strips
1 teaspoon pickling spice

In small pan, combine all ingredients and heat to boiling. Remove and chill. Serves 4-6.

*Per serving: 54 calories; 0.2 fat grams*

 If cooking fresh beets, leave about an inch of the stem so color will not bleed.

# BROCCOLI SALAD

*Georgie and Cyndi both have friends who served this to them several years ago; raisins and sunflower seeds make it unusual.*

2 heads broccoli, separated, cut in small
    pieces
1 pound bacon, cooked crisp and crumbled
1 small red onion, chopped
1/2 cup raisins
1 cup unsalted sunflower kernels


Dressing:
1 cup light mayonnaise
2 tablespoons red wine vinegar
1/2 cup sugar

In large bowl, combine all ingredients. Add dressing and mix well. Refrigerate until ready to serve. Serves 10-12.


Dressing:
In small bowl, combine ingredients. Pour over broccoli mixture and mix well.


*Per serving: 361 calories; 25.0 fat grams*

# BROCCOLI SLAW

*Amazingly easy.*

1/3 cup light salad dressing or light
    mayonnaise
1/4 cup cider vinegar
4 teaspoons sugar
2 teaspoons celery seeds
1 bunch watercress
1 16-ounce package broccoli coleslaw or
    shredded cabbage mix for coleslaw

In large bowl, mix mayonnaise, vinegar, sugar and celery seeds together. Add watercress and slaw mixture. Toss. Serves 4.

*Per serving: 76 calories; 1.7 fat grams*

 Prepackaged coleslaw mix makes this salad easy, but feel free to shred your own.

# COLESLAW

*Celery seed accents the flavor of the cabbage in this coleslaw.*

3 cups cabbage, shredded
1/4 cup green pepper, chopped
2 tablespoons onion, chopped
3 tablespoons oil
3 tablespoons red wine vinegar
1 teaspoon celery seed
1 teaspoon sugar

In large bowl, toss cabbage, green pepper and onion together. In container with lid, combine oil, vinegar, celery seed and sugar; shake well to mix. Pour dressing over cabbage mixture and toss. Serves 4-6.

*Per serving: 88 calories; 8.3 fat grams*

For a creamy coleslaw, eliminate oil and add 1/3 cup mayonnaise, sour cream or ranch dressing.

# GRANDPA JAY'S CUCUMBER SALAD

3/4 cup sour cream
Dash pepper
1 tablespoon mayonnaise
2 medium cucumbers, peeled & sliced
1 small onion, sliced thin

In small bowl, combine sour cream, pepper and mayonnaise. Mix well. Combine cucumbers and onion slices. Add sour cream mixture and stir. Serves 4.

*Per serving: 45 calories; 1.3 fat grams*

**Foot Note** Georgie's mom, Geneva, told us that the mayonnaise was added to prevent the sour cream from becoming watery.

# SAUERKRAUT SALAD

*In Cyndi's opinion this is best served with brats or German sausage. The Patrick family favorite is a combination of Polish sausage and pirogi.*

1 27-ounce can sauerkraut, drained
1 large green pepper, chopped
1 large onion, chopped
1 cup celery, diced
1 2-ounce jar pimento, chopped
1 1/2 cups sugar
1/2 cup vegetable oil
1/2 cup vinegar

Mix all ingredients well. Refrigerate 24 hours.
Serves 8-10.

*Per serving: 262 calories; 12.3 fat grams*

For a different taste, cut the sugar to 1 cup and use the Bavarian style sauerkraut.

*Salads*

# FRESH SPINACH SALAD

6 cups fresh spinach, torn
2 tablespoons olive oil
1 tablespoon lemon juice
8 slices bacon, fried crisp
3 hard boiled eggs, chopped

Dressing
1/2 teaspoon dry mustard
1 teaspoon salt
1/2 teaspoon paprika
1 tablespoon sugar
1 teaspoon Worcestershire sauce
1 cup oil
1/2 cup red wine vinegar
1/2 cup warm water

In large bowl, toss spinach with olive oil and lemon juice. Just before serving, add bacon and eggs. Toss with dressing. Serves 6-8.

Dressing
In medium mixing bowl, beat mustard, salt, paprika, sugar and Worcestershire sauce together. Combine oil, vinegar and water in large cup and slowly beat into mixture. Beat until slightly thickened. Refrigerate until ready to use.

*Per serving: 397 calories; 40.7 fat grams*

# SPINACH SALAD WITH COTTAGE CHEESE DRESSING

1 pound fresh spinach, torn
1 head iceberg lettuce, torn
1/2 pound bacon, fried crisp and crumbled

Dressing
1/2 cup sugar
1 teaspoon salt
1 teaspoon dry mustard
1 tablespoon onion flakes
1/2 cup cider vinegar
1 cup oil
1 tablespoon poppy seeds
1 1/2 cups small curd, light cottage cheese

In large bowl, combine and toss together with dressing.  Serves 12.

Dressing
Combine all ingredients in a container with a lid. Cover and shake well.

*Per serving: 345 calories; 28.6 fat grams*

# SPINACH-SPROUT SALAD

6 cups fresh spinach, washed and torn
6 cups assorted salad greens, washed and
    torn
1 8-ounce can bean sprouts, drained

Dressing
1/2 cup oil
1/4 cup red wine vinegar
1/2 teaspoon lemon peel
1/2 teaspoon soy sauce
1/2 teaspoon honey
Dash pepper

Combine in large bowl. Just before serving toss with dressing. Serves 12

Dressing
Combine all ingredients in container with lid. Cover and shake well. Refrigerate until ready to serve.

*Per serving: 96 calories; 9.2 fat grams*

# KOREAN SALAD

6 cups fresh spinach, washed and torn
1 8-ounce can water chestnuts, drained and
    rinsed
1 10-ounce can bean sprouts, drained and
    rinsed
1 medium onion, quartered and thinly
    sliced
3 hard-boiled eggs, diced
5 strips bacon, cooked crisp and broken

Dressing:
3/4 cup vegetable oil
1/2 cup sugar
1/3 cup catsup
1/4 cup vinegar
1 tablespoon Worcestershire Sauce
1/2 teaspoon salt

In large bowl, combine all ingredients. Toss with dressing. Serves 8-10.

Dressing:
In container with lid, combine all ingredients and shake well to mix.

*Per serving: 288 calories; 15.6 fat grams*

# SESAME SPINACH SALAD

3 tablespoons sesame seeds
2 heads Romaine lettuce, washed and torn
3 cups fresh spinach, washed and torn
3 tomatoes, peeled and coarsely diced
1/2 cup green onions, sliced
2 cups seasoned croutons

Dressing:
1 tablespoon Worcestershire Sauce
3 tablespoons vinegar
1 tablespoon honey
1/2 teaspoon dry mustard

In small fry pan sprayed with cooking oil, saute sesame seeds to light brown. Cool. In large bowl, combine all ingredients, except croutons and sesame seeds. Toss with dressing. Add croutons and sesame seeds; toss. Serves 8-10.

Dressing:
In container with lid, combine all ingredients; shake well.

*Per serving: 100 calories; 3.8 fat grams*

# WILTED LETTUCE

*We all have probably eaten this wonderful salad at Grandmother's.*

4 slices bacon
2 tablespoons bacon drippings
1/4 cup white vinegar
2 tablespoons water
1 head red leaf lettuce, torn
2 teaspoons sugar
2 green onions, sliced
Salt and pepper to taste

In small skillet, fry bacon until crisp, saving drippings for dressing; crumble in pan. Add vinegar and water. Simmer on low until ready to pour on lettuce. In large bowl, toss lettuce, sugar, onions, salt and pepper together. Pour bacon mixture over lettuce, toss and serve immediately. Serves 4.

*Per serving: 132 calories; 9.9 fat grams*

Foot Notes

Variation:

1/4 cup unsweetened pineapple juice
2 tablespoons white vinegar
2 teaspoons olive oil
1/2 teaspoon soy sauce
1/4 teaspoon dry mustard
1/8 teaspoon curry powder
1/8 teaspoon pepper

In small pan, bring all ingredients to boil. Pour over lettuce and toss. Serve immediately.

# ITALIAN TOSSED SALAD

*Serve this salad with your favorite Italian meal. It is so easy.*

6 cups lettuce
2 tomatoes, cut into wedges
1 4-ounce can garbanzo beans
1/2 cup shredded Mozzarella cheese
10 slices pepperoni, quartered
1 8-ounce bottled Italian dressing

In large bowl, combine all ingredients and toss. Serves 6.

*Per serving: 185 calories; 12.6 fat grams*

 Experiment with your own favorite combination of greens, vegetables and cheeses to make delicious tossed salads.

# TRAIL MIX SALAD

1 head iceberg lettuce, torn
2 11-ounce cans mandarin oranges, drained
1/2 cup trail mix (available in bulk at gro-
    cery stores, or make your own combi-
    nation of dried fruit and nuts

Dressing
1/2 cup honey
1/2 cup cider vinegar
1/3 cup poppy seeds
1 8-ounce jar brown mustard
1/2 teaspoon salt
1 cup oil

In large bowl, combine lettuce, oranges and trail mix. Add dressing and toss. Serves 6-8.

Dressing
In blender, whirl honey, vinegar, poppy seeds, mustard and salt. Slowly add oil and continue to blend until thick.

*Per person: 434 calories; 32.3 fat grams*

# CHEF'S SALAD

*This is an awesome, low fat dressing that is a Cyndi creation. She likes it so much that she uses it on tortilla roll-ups, sandwiches, toast or anything she can.*

8 cups iceberg lettuce, torn
2 cups cooked roast beef, turkey or ham,
    cut in strips, or a combination
2 hard-boiled eggs, cut in quarters
2 ounces Swiss cheese, cut in strips
2 tomatoes, cut in wedges
1/2 cup radishes, sliced
1/4 cucumber, thinly sliced
1/2 cup black olives, optional
1 small red onion, sliced, separated

Dressing
1 cup fresh spinach
3 tablespoons onion, optional
1/4 medium cucumber
1/4 cup green pepper
1 teaspoon salt
1/2 teaspoon pepper
1 teaspoon dry mustard
6 tablespoons white vinegar
1/3 cup oil

On 4 dinner plates, divide lettuce evenly. Arrange remaining ingredients attractively on top. Serve favorite dressing separately. Serves 4.

Dressing
Place all ingredients in blender; whirl at high speed 2 minutes. Makes 1 1/2 cups dressing. Double, if desired.

*Per serving:*
*Beef: 588 calories; 37.0 fat grams*
*Turkey: 433 calories; 32.0 fat grams*
*Ham: 414 calories; 30.5 fat grams*

# SEVEN-LAYER SALAD

*We had to include this all-time favorite, due to popular demand. The recipe has been around a long time and is easy to prepare.*

1 head iceberg lettuce, torn
1/2 cup celery, chopped
1 cup green pepper, chopped
1 red onion, chopped
1 10-ounce package frozen peas, thawed
2 cups light salad dressing or light mayon-
    naise
2 tablespoons sugar
2 cups cheddar cheese, grated
1 pound bacon, cooked crisp, crumbled

In 10 x 13 x 2 pan, layer first five ingredients (do not mix). Cover with salad dressing, being sure to seal around edges. Sprinkle sugar over mayonnaise, cover with cheese and spread bacon pieces over top. Cover and refrigerate overnight. Serves 8-10.

*Per serving: 546 calories; 51.8 fat grams*

 For quicker preparation, substitute 1/2 to 3/4 cup bacon bits for cooked bacon.

# MIXED VEGETABLE SALAD

*Use an ice bucket for an attractive serving container that also keeps the food cool.*

1/4 cup low calorie French salad dressing
1/4 cup light salad dressing or mayonnaise
2 tablespoons chili sauce
2 teaspoons lemon juice
1 teaspoon salt
1/8 teaspoon pepper
2 16-ounce packages frozen Italian mixed
    vegetables, cooked and drained
1/2 cup celery, chopped
1/4 cup onion, chopped

In small bowl, combine salad dressings, chili sauce, lemon juice, salt and pepper. Mix well. In large bowl, combine all vegetables. Add dressing; toss to coat. Serves 8.

*Per serving: 73 calories; 1.4 fat grams*

To speed up this recipe, cook frozen vegetables in microwave (in large microwavable dish, combine vegetables; add 2-3 tablespoons water. Cook on high 8 minutes, stirring three times).

# BEAN SALAD

*This colorful salad is always a quick favorite for potluck dinners and almost always found on restaurant salad bars.*

1 16-ounce can red kidney beans
1 16-ounce can green beans
1 16-ounce can yellow beans
1 medium red onion, chopped
1 cup green pepper, chopped
1/4 cup pimento, chopped, optional
1/2 cup sugar
1/2 cup red wine vinegar
1/2 cup oil

Drain and rinse all beans in colander. Transfer to large bowl. Add remaining ingredients and toss together. Refrigerate overnight to enhance flavor. Serves 12-15.

*Per serving: 268 calories; 9.9 fat grams*

Cyndi likes to add garbanzo beans to this salad. For a little variation, use garlic vinegar.

# THREE BEAN-AVOCADO SALAD

1 16-ounce can pinto beans
1 16-ounce can kidney beans
1 10-ounce can garbanzo beans
1 tablespoon pimento, chopped
1/4 cup green onions, sliced
1/2 cup oil
1/4 cup red wine vinegar
1/4 cup lemon juice
2 tablespoons sugar
3/4 teaspoon chili powder
1/2 teaspoon salt
1/8 teaspoon garlic salt
1/8 teaspoon pepper
Lettuce
3 to 4 avocados, sliced

Drain and rinse all beans; pour into large bowl. Add pimento and onions. In large container with lid, combine oil, vinegar, lemon juice, sugar, chili powder, salt, garlic salt and pepper; shake to mix well. Pour over beans. Chill until ready to serve. Arrange lettuce on platter or individual salad plates. Place avocados on lettuce. Spoon bean salad over avocados. Serves 8-10.

*Per serving: 371 calories; 11.3 fat grams*

Substitute a combination of your favorite beans to give this salad a different flavor.

Avocados should be prepared just before serving to keep them from discoloring.

# RED KIDNEY BEAN SALAD

*Cyndi remembers this salad being served often as a youngster.*

1 15-ounce can kidney beans, drained and
   rinsed
3 hard-boiled eggs, diced
1/2 cup sweet relish
1 teaspoon celery seed
Salt and pepper to taste
3/4-1 cup light salad dressing or mayonnaise

In medium bowl, combine all ingredients and toss.
Serves 4-5.

*Per serving: 177 calories; 5.0 fat grams*

Eating 1/2 cup of beans daily is a good way to lower cholesterol by 10%.

# MILLIONAIRE SALAD

1 medium head cauliflower, separated
1 bunch broccoli, separated
1 pint fresh mushrooms, sliced
1 cup celery, sliced
1 medium zucchini, sliced
1 2-ounce jar chopped pimento
1 16-ounce bottle light or fat free Italian
   dressing

In large bowl, combine all ingredients.  Refrigerate overnight.  Serves 10-12.

*Per serving: 54 calories; 4.2 fat grams*

 Although the recipe calls for overnight refrigeration of this salad, it is also wonderful served immediately after preparation.

# LUCILLE'S CAULIFLOWER SALAD

*This is another favorite that Cyndi's mom makes. It's easy and makes a delicious leftover salad.*

1/2 head cauliflower, separated in small
    pieces
1 head broccoli, separated in small pieces
1 green pepper, chopped
3 stalks celery, sliced
1 cup colby cheese, diced
1 6-ounce jar stuffed green olives
1 8-ounce bottle coleslaw dressing

In large salad bowl, combine all ingredients, except dressing. Refrigerate until ready to serve. Toss with dressing. Serves 12.

*Per serving: 132 calories; 10.9 fat grams*

If you have leftover salad, add it to lettuce to make a quick tossed salad. Additional dressing is not necessary.

# CAULIFLOWER AND BROCCOLI SALAD

1 small head cauliflower, cut up
1 small head broccoli, cut up
1 red onion or 6 green onions, chopped

Dressing
1/3 cup vinegar
1/3 cup oil
1/3 cup sugar
1/3 cup light mayonnaise
Salt and pepper to taste

Combine in large bowl.  Pour dressing over ingredients and mix.  Serves 8.

Dressing
Combine all ingredients in container with lid. Cover and shake well.   Pour over salad.

*Per serving: 135 calories; 9.7 fat grams*

# PEA SALAD

*This recipe can be easily doubled.*

1 16-ounce can peas, drained, or 2 cups
    frozen peas
3 hard-boiled eggs, chopped
1 onion, chopped
4 small sweet pickles, chopped
1/4 cup salted peanuts
1 2-ounce jar pimentos
1/4 teaspoon salt
1/4 teaspoon pepper
3 tablespoons light salad dressing or
    mayonnaise

In medium bowl, combine all ingredients and mix gently. Refrigerate until ready to serve. Serves 4-6.

*Per serving: 166 calories; 8.1 fat grams*

# GRANDMA D'S PEA SALAD

*Dinners at "home" were not complete without this simple, but wonderful, salad.*

1 16-ounce can peas, drained
1 medium onion, chopped
1/4 pound cheddar cheese, diced
2 dill pickles, chopped over bowl to save
    juice
1 2-ounce jar pimento
3 hard-boiled eggs, chopped
Salt and pepper to taste

In medium bowl, mix all ingredients together.

*Per serving: 169 calories; 10.4 fat grams*

 To hard boil eggs Cyndi and Georgie's way, place eggs in pan and cover with cold water. Bring to a boil, reduce heat to medium and continue cooking for 15 minutes. This reduces cracking. A cloth can also be placed in the bottom of the pan to prevent eggs from breaking. Always boil extra eggs for later use.

# GREEK SALAD

1 head romaine lettuce
1 small green pepper, thinly sliced
1 small red onion, thinly sliced
1 tomato, chopped
2 ounces feta cheese, crumbled

Dressing:
2 tablespoons red wine vinegar
1 tablespoon oil
1/8 teaspoon pepper
1 clove garlic, crushed

In large bowl, combine lettuce, pepper, onion and tomato. Pour dressing over salad and toss. Top with feta cheese. Serves 6.

Dressing:
Combine all ingredients in container with lid and shake well.

*Per serving: 76 calories; 4.6 fat grams*

# FETA CHEESE SALAD WITH ANCHOVIES

1 medium head iceberg lettuce, chopped
1 head curly endive, chopped
2 tomatoes, cut in wedges
1/2 cup pitted ripe olives
1/4 cup green onions, sliced
2/3 cup olive oil
1/3 cup red wine vinegar
1/2 teaspoon salt
1/4 teaspoon oregano
1/8 teaspoon pepper
3 ounces feta cheese, cubed
1 3-ounce can anchovy fillets, drained,
　　optional

In large bowl, toss greens.  Place tomato, olives and onions on top of greens.  In a container with lid, combine oil, vinegar, salt, oregano and pepper.  Cover and shake well to mix.  Pour over salad.  Top with cheese and anchovies.  Serves 12.

*Per serving: 163 calories; 15.0 fat grams*

Cream cheese can be substituted for the feta cheese if that's what you have available.

Substitute leftover grilled steak strips for the anchovies.

# COLD GRILLED VEGGIE SALAD

1 red onion, sliced
6-8 stalks fresh asparagus
1 1/2 cups fresh mushrooms
1 yellow squash, sliced
1 medium zucchini, sliced
1 medium red pepper, sliced
1 medium yellow pepper, sliced

Dressing
1/3 cup white vinegar
1/4 cup oil
1/4 teaspoon garlic powder
1/2 teaspoon dry mustard
1 teaspoon thyme or basil, or combination
   of both
3 tablespoons sugar
1/4 teaspoon salt
1/4 teaspoon pepper

Put vegetables in wire grilling hopper. Cook over medium coals for 10 minutes, turning 3-4 times during cooking time. Prepare dressing and pour over salad. Cover and refrigerate until ready to serve. Serves 4-6.

Dressing
Combine all ingredients in container with lid, cover and shake to mix thoroughly.

*Per serving: 176 calories; 11.3 fat grams*

# PATRICK POTATO SALAD

*This potato salad is not the same with mayonnaise or brown mustard.*

6 large potatoes, cooked and diced
4 hard-boiled eggs, diced
1/2 onion, chopped
1 cup salad dressing
2 teaspoons prepared mustard
1/4 cup sweet pickle relish
Salt and pepper to taste

In large bowl, mix all ingredients together. Stir well. Garnish with sliced hard-boiled eggs and paprika. Serves 4-6.

*Per serving: 336 calories; 19.6 fat grams*

Georgie prefers this salad served warm and the potatoes very soft. Her family prefers it cold.

# SOUR CREAM POTATO SALAD

*The addition of celery seed and cucumber makes this recipe different from other potato salads.*

6 cups potatoes, cooked and diced
1 teaspoon salt
1/2 cup cucumber, finely diced
1 tablespoon onion, finely chopped
1 teaspoon celery seed
6 hard-boiled eggs
3/4 cup light sour cream
3/4 cup light mayonnaise
2 tablespoons vinegar
1 teaspoon prepared mustard

In large bowl, lightly toss potatoes, salt, cucumber, onion and celery seed. Remove whites from hard-boiled eggs and add to potato mixture. In medium bowl, mash egg yolks; combine with sour cream, mayonnaise, vinegar and mustard. Mix thoroughly and fold into potato mixture. Chill well. Serve over salad greens with favorite grilled meat. Serves 8.

*Per serving: 116 calories; 5.2 fat grams*

# HOT GERMAN POTATO SALAD

*This is a Duncan favorite.*

9 potatoes, sliced
1 3/4 cups water
1 onion, chopped
2 tablespoons flour
2 tablespoons sugar
1 teaspoon salt
Dash of pepper
1/2 teaspoon celery seed
1/3 cup vinegar
6 slices bacon, cooked crisp (We cook
    bacon in the microwave)

In large fry pan, combine 1 cup water, potatoes and onion. Cover and cook 20 minutes. Meanwhile, mix flour, sugar, salt, celery seed, 3/4 cup water and vinegar together in small bowl. Pour over potato mixture. Cover and simmer 10 more minutes. Stir in bacon. Serve with grilled Brats, sauerkraut and rye bread. Serves 6.

*Per serving: 169 calories; 3.3 fat grams*

Use leftover baked or boiled potatoes, or microwave the potatoes for quick preparation.

# HERBED TOMATOES

6 large ripe tomatoes, peeled and cut into thick slices

Dressing:
1 teaspoon salt
1/4 teaspoon coarse black pepper
1 teaspoon thyme or marjoram, or combination of favorite herbs
1/4 cup fresh parsley, finely snipped, or 2 teaspoons dried parsley
1/4 cup chives, snipped, or 2 teaspoons dried chives
2/3 cup oil
1/4 cup tarragon vinegar
Lettuce leaves

Dressing:
In small bowl, combine all ingredients, except tomatoes and lettuce leaves. In 9" x 13" dish, overlap tomatoes. Gently pour dressing over tomatoes. Refrigerate. To serve, place lettuce leaves on 6 salad plates; using slotted spoon, lift tomatoes onto lettuce leaves. Serves 6.

*Per serving: 114 calories; 9.5 fat grams*

This also makes a great dressing for cherry tomatoes, broccoli and cauliflower salad. Think about substituting green and red peppers, zucchini and yellow squash for tomatoes.

*Salads*

# AMBROSIA

*There are so many versions of this salad, but this one is our favorite.*

1 cup flaked coconut
1 cup miniature marshmallows
1 cup whipped topping
1 cup sour cream
1 cup strawberries, sliced
1 banana, sliced
1 11-ounce can mandarin oranges
1 cup pineapple tidbits, well drained
12 maraschino cherries, halved, optional
1/4 cup almonds for garnish

In large bowl, mix together coconut, marshmallows, whipped topping and sour cream. Add fruit and gently mix. Chill. Garnish with almonds. Serves 8.

*Per serving: 566 calories; 5.7 fat grams*

 Create your own ambrosia by varying fruits and nuts. Frozen or canned fruit can be substituted when fresh fruit is not in season.

# HONEY FRUIT CUPS

*Great for a buffet. Try serving as fruit parfaits, layering fruit and honey mixture in tall glasses.*

4 cups fresh fruit of choice, cut up
1 6-ounce carton mandarin orange, vanilla
    or lemon yogurt
1 tablespoon honey
1/2 teaspoon grated orange peel
1/4 teaspoon almond extract

In small bowl, combine yogurt, honey, orange peel and extract. Arrange fruit on platter with bowl of honey mixture in center. Guests can spoon honey mixture over their own serving of fruit. Serves 4.

*Per serving: 113 calories; 0.9 fat grams*

**Foot Note**

Orange Fruit Dip:
Combine 1 3 1/2-ounce package instant vanilla pudding mix and 3/4 cup milk in container with lid. Shake for 3 minutes. Stir in 1/2 teaspoon orange peel and 1/4 cup orange juice. Serve as a fruit dip.

# CHINESE FRUIT SALAD

1 10-ounce package frozen pea pods
1/2 cup walnuts
1 tablespoon butter or margarine
1 head iceberg lettuce, torn
1/2 red onion, sliced
1 6-ounce can sliced water chestnuts, drained
1 11-ounce can mandarin oranges, drained
1 11-ounce can chunk pineapple, drained

Dressing:
1 tablespoon oil
2 tablespoons sesame seeds
3 tablespoons lemon juice, fresh or bottled
1 tablespoon sugar

In microwave dish, microwave pea pods 2-3 minutes on high. Rinse in cold water to cool. In small fry pan, saute walnuts in butter for 3-4 minutes. Set aside to cool. In large bowl, combine all ingredients. Add dressing and toss. Serves 6-8.

Dressing:
In container with lid, combine all ingredients, cover and shake well.

*Per serving: 140 calories; 6.6 fat grams*

For a different flavored dressing, saute sesame seeds in oil until golden. Stir in lemon juice and sugar.

# MOM HERRING'S FRUIT SALAD

*Harriet's family still enjoys this salad for Thanksgiving dinner, a tradition started by her mother.*

1 11-ounce can mandarin oranges, drained
1 20-ounce can chunk pineapple, drained,
    reserve juice
3 or 4 bananas, sliced
2 red apples, chopped
1 cup red grapes, halved
3 kiwi, sliced
1 1/2 cups miniature marshmallows
1 cup pecans, chopped

Dressing:
1/2 cup reserved pineapple juice
1/4 cup lemon juice or fresh juice from
    large lemon
2 tablespoons sugar
1 egg, beaten

Prepare dressing first and allow to cool while preparing fruit. In large bowl, combine all ingredients. Cover with cooled dressing and mix. Refrigerate 3-4 hours or until ready to serve. Serves 12-15.

Dressing:
In medium pan, heat juices and sugar until sugar is dissolved. In bowl with beaten egg, slowly stir in 2-3 tablespoons hot liquid. Pour into pan with rest of liquid. Cook and stir over low heat until smooth. Cool before putting on salad.

*Per serving: 157 calories; 4.0 fat grams*

# ORANGE-DATE WALDORF

1 orange, peeled and halve sections
1 tablespoon orange juice (hold orange over
    small bowl while sectioning to catch
    juice)
2 cups unpeeled apple, diced
1/2 cup pitted dates, chopped
1/2 cup celery, chopped
1/3 cup walnuts, coarsely chopped
1/4 cup light salad dressing or mayonnaise
1 tablespoon sugar
3/4 cup whipped topping
Lettuce leaves

In large bowl, combine orange, apple, dates, celery and walnuts. In small bowl, mix together salad dressing, sugar and orange juice. Fold in whipped topping. Lightly toss with fruit. On 6 individual salad plates, spoon salad on top of lettuce leaves. Serves 6.

*Per serving: 118 calories; 2.9 fat grams*

# LAST MINUTE FRUIT SALAD

1 15-ounce can spiced peaches in heavy
   syrup
1 11-ounce can pineapple chunks
1 apple, thinly sliced
1 cup strawberries, sliced
1 banana, sliced
1 cup red and/or green grapes
1 11-ounce can mandarin oranges, drained
2 tablespoons vanilla or peach yogurt

In large bowl, combine all ingredients. Mix well.
Serves 8-10.

*Per serving: 101 calories; 0.4 fat grams*

# MOM'S CRANBERRY SALAD

*Cyndi's mom makes this salad at Christmas time at everyone's request even though we have Mexican food instead of the traditional turkey or ham dinner.*

1 16-ounce package fresh cranberries,
   washed and ground
1 whole orange with peel, washed and
   ground
1 8-ounce can crushed pineapple
1 stalk celery, chopped, optional
1/2 cup walnuts, finely chopped, optional
1 3-ounce package raspberry, cherry or
   strawberry gelatin
1 cup boiling water
1 1/2 cups sugar

In large bowl, combine all ingredients. Mix and refrigerate until firm. Serves 10.

*Per serving: 211 calories; 1.1 fat grams*

 Foot Notes

Although Lucille uses an old fashioned grinder to grind cranberries and orange, a blender or food processor works just as well.

This salad could be put into individual molds or a large mold for a more festive look.

# CRANBERRY CHUNK SALAD

2 3-ounce packages cream cheese at room
   temperature, softened
1/4 cup light salad dressing or light
   mayonnaise
1/4 cup lemon juice
2 tablespoons sugar
1/8 teaspoon salt
1 cup crushed pineapple, drained
1 cup walnuts, chopped
1 cup bananas, diced
1 1/2 cups heavy cream, whipped until stiff
1 16-ounce can jellied cranberry sauce, cut
   into chunks

In mixer bowl, beat cream cheese, mayonnaise,
lemon juice, sugar and salt until smooth. Stir in
pineapple, walnuts and bananas. Fold in whipped
cream. Add cranberry chunks and gently fold.
Pour mixture into serving bowl, mold or small individual serving dishes. Refrigerate until ready to
serve. Serves 12.

*Per serving: 262 calories; 17.8 fat grams*

Try freezing this salad. Place in
refrigerator about 30 minutes
before serving. Remove from
mold(s), and serve atop a fresh lettuce leaf.

# TANGY FIESTA FRUIT BOWL

*When served in a clear glass bowl, this is an attractive addition to any buffet. Vary it with a personal choice of fruits.*

1 cantaloupe melon, halved and seeded
1/2 honeydew melon, seeded
1/4 cup sugar
1/4 cup lime juice
1 1/2 teaspoons lime peel, grated
2 tablespoons lemon juice
1 cup fresh strawberries, sliced
1 cup black or red seedless grapes

Use a melon baller to make melon balls; put in large bowl and set aside. In a large non-metal bowl, combine sugar, lime juice, lemon juice and lime peel. Stir until sugar is dissolved. Add fruit and toss gently to cover all fruit with juices. Cover and refrigerate for at least 1 hour to blend flavors, stirring once or twice. To serve spoon into large glass bowl, or spoon into decorative, hollowed-out melon halves. Serves 8.

*Per serving: 70 calories; 0.3 fat grams*

Foot Notes

To make melon basket, draw zig-zag pattern on melon with non-toxic marker. Using a long knife, cut along pattern, separate halves and seed. If you are really artistic, make a handle without separating halves. Remove remainder of melon. Fill cavity with fruit, chicken salad, cottage cheese or ice cream.

If serving on a flat dish, cut slice off bottom so melon will stay level.

*Salads*

# FRESH FRUIT SALAD

*Oh, so good during the summer when fresh fruit is plentiful.*

6 cups mixed fruit, cut up (apple, melon,
    orange, grapefruit, strawberries, pear,
    banana, grapes)
1 cup shredded coconut, optional
1 cup nuts, chopped, optional
1 kiwi, sliced
Lettuce leaves

Dressing:
1 cup vanilla yogurt
2 tablespoons frozen orange juice concentrate

In a large bowl, combine fruit, coconut and nuts. Mix with dressing and chill. Serve on lettuce leaves. Garnish with kiwi slices. Serves 12.

Dressing:
Blend yogurt and orange juice concentrate.

*Per serving: 253 calories; 8.3 fat grams*

 Try this peanut butter dressing on fresh fruit salads: In mixer bowl, combine 1 cup marshmallow cream and 1/4 cup orange juice; beat until fluffy. Add 1/2 cup peanut butter, 1/4 cup light mayonnaise and 1 tablespoon lemon juice and mix. Serve over fresh or canned fruit. Serves 8-12.

*Per serving: 121 calories; 6.8 fat grams*

# FRUIT SALAD ICE

1 17-ounce can apricots, drained and diced, reserving liquid
1 17-ounce can crushed pineapple, drained, reserving liquid
1 cup liquid from fruits; adding water if necessary
1/2 cup sugar
3 10-ounce packages frozen strawberries
1 6-ounce can frozen orange juice
2 tablespoons lemon juice
3 bananas, diced

In large bowl, combine liquid and sugar; microwave for 1 minute. Stir until sugar dissolves. Add apricots, pineapple, strawberries, orange juice, lemon juice and bananas. Mix. Place cupcake papers in muffin tins. Spoon fruit mixture into papers. Freeze until solid. Within 20 minutes of serving time, set out to thaw slightly. Serves 12-15.

*Per serving: 150 calories; 0.3 fat grams*

Cups of fruit salad can be frozen and then stored in plastic bags in the freezer.

# SUNSHINE SALAD

1/8 cup oil
Juice from 1/2 lemon
2 teaspoons lemon peel, grated
1 tablespoon sugar
1 tablespoon parsley
1/4 teaspoon dried dill
4 navel oranges, peeled, thinly sliced
1 red onion, sliced
Red leafy lettuce

In medium bowl, combine oil, lemon juice, lemon peel, sugar, parsley and dill. Mix well. Add oranges and onion. Toss. Arrange lettuce leaves on 4 salad plates. Spoon salad on top of lettuce. Serves 4.

*Per serving: 143 calories; 7.3 fat grams*

 Grate extra lemon and orange peel; store in sealed plastic bags in the freezer.

# APRICOT DELIGHT

*Renee satisfies her family's requests by making delicious gelatin salads. Since it is a layered gelatin salad and requires time for each layer to set, it is not necessarily a quick recipe.*

1 29-ounce can apricots, drained and
    reserved, cut up finely
1 29-ounce can crushed pineapple, drained
    and reserved
2 3-ounce packages orange or apricot, or
    one of each, gelatin
2 cups boiling water
3/4 cup miniature marshmallows
1 cup apricot and pineapple juice

Topping:
1/2 cup sugar
3 tablespoons flour
1 egg, beaten
1 cup reserved fruit juice
2 tablespoons butter
1 cup whipped topping
1/2 cup cheddar cheese, grated

Chill fruits and juice while preparing gelatin. In large bowl, dissolve gelatin in boiling water. Add 1 cup of fruit juice; stir well. Refrigerate until slightly gelled. Fold in fruit and marshmallows. Pour into 13 x 9 x 2 dish. Chill until firm. Meanwhile, prepare topping. Cut in squares. Serves 9-12 depending on cut.

Topping:
In small pan, combine sugar, flour and egg. Gradually stir in juice. Cook over low heat until thickened, stirring constantly. Remove from heat, stir in butter and cool. Fold in topping. Spread over firm gelatin and sprinkle with cheese. Refrigerate until ready to serve.

*Per serving: 282 calories; 5.8 fat grams*

*Salads*

# CHERRY COLA SALAD

*The combination of cola and sour cherries puts a zing in this salad.*

2 boxes cherry-flavored gelatin
1 16-ounce red sour pitted cherries
1 cup sugar
1/2 cup water
1 11-ounce can crushed pineapple
1 cup walnuts, chopped
1 12-ounce can cola

In large saucepan, bring cherries with juice, water and sugar to a boil. Add gelatin, stirring until dissolved. Refrigerate until partially set. Stir in pineapple, nuts and cold cola. Pour into mold. Refrigerate until set. Serves 8-10.

*Per serving: 237 calories; 2.1 fat grams*

 Gelatin will set up faster if placed in freezer for a few minutes, or use the quick method on the gelatin package.

# RASPBERRY APPLESAUCE SALAD

*Georgie's friend Sally gave her this recipe, and it has been a Patrick favorite ever since.*

1 3-ounce box raspberry gelatin
1 1/4 cups hot water
1 1/4 cups applesauce
1 10-ounce package frozen raspberries,
    thawed
1 cup miniature marshmallows
1 cup sour cream

Dissolve gelatin in hot water. Stir in applesauce and raspberries. Pour into 9 x 13 glass dish. Refrigerate until firmly set. In small mixing bowl, combine marshmallows and sour cream. Spread over gelatin mixture. Refrigerate. Cut into squares to serve. Serves 10-12.

*Per serving: 99 calories; 0.5 fat grams*

 Make this salad ahead of time. Just before serving. spread on the marsh-mallows with sour cream.

# FROSTED LEMON GELATIN

*The cooked topping on this salad/dessert sets it apart from the traditional fruit gelatin.*

1 4-ounce can crushed pineapple, drained,
　　reserving juice
2 cups boiling water
2 3-ounce packages lemon gelatin
2 cups carbonated lemon-lime drink
3 bananas, diced
1 cup miniature marshmallows
1 1/2 cups whipped topping

Topping:
1/2 cup pineapple juice
1 egg, slightly beaten
1/2 cup sugar
1 tablespoon flour

In 9" x 13" dish, place gelatin. Add boiling water and stir until gelatin is dissolved. Add lemon-lime drink and stir. Add bananas and marshmallows. Refrigerate until set. Spread with topping and frost with whipped topping. Cut in squares to serve. Serves 8-10.

Topping:
In small pan, combine ingredients. Cook over medium heat until thickened. Cool.

*Per serving: 200 calories; 2.3 fat grams*

# QUICK TOMATO ASPIC

1 3-ounce package lemon gelatin
1 1/4 cups boiling water
1 8-ounce can Italian seasoned tomato
    sauce
1 tablespoon cider vinegar
1/2 teaspoon seasoned salt
Salt and fresh ground pepper to taste
Lettuce

In medium bowl, dissolve gelatin in boiling water; add remaining ingredients. Pour into individual molds. Chill until firm. Unmold onto 4 lettuce leaf lined salad plates. Serves 4.

*Per serving: 93 calories; 0.2 fat grams*

Mold in 10-ounce soup cans; unmold and slice as you would canned cranberry sauce.

# FIESTA TOSS

1 pound lean ground beef
1 15-ounce can kidney beans, drained
1/4 teaspoon salt
1 head iceberg lettuce, torn
1 red onion, chopped
4 tomatoes, cut up
4 ounces cheddar cheese, grated
1 8-ounce bottle light Thousand Island
    dressing
5-6 drops hot pepper sauce to taste
1 10-ounce package corn chips, crushed

In large skillet, brown ground beef; drain. Add beans and salt. Simmer 10 minutes, then cool slightly. Meanwhile, in large bowl, place lettuce, tomatoes, onion and cheese. Toss with salad dressing and hot sauce. Add meat and corn chips just before serving. Toss lightly. Serves 6 to 8.

*Per serving: 739 calories; 36.7 fat grams*

Foot Note

Instead of using corn chips, make tortilla strips: roll up 2 10-inch tortillas and cut into thin slices. Toss strips with 2 tablespoons Italian or ranch dressing; scatter strips on baking sheet and bake at 375° 5 to 8 minutes until lightly browned and crisp. Cool then toss with salad.

# TERIYAKI STEAK SALAD

1 1-pound beef flank steak
1/2 teaspoon salt
1/2 teaspoon freshly ground pepper
1/4 cup teriyaki sauce
3 tablespoons olive oil
2 tablespoons light mayonnaise
1 tablespoon Dijon mustard
1 tablespoon lemon juice
1 garlic clove, finely minced
1/3 cup fresh parmesan cheese, grated
1 medium head romaine lettuce, torn
1 medium head red leaf lettuce, torn
1 medium cucumber, thinly sliced

Preheat grill or broiler. Place steak on grill or boiler pan. Sprinkle with salt and pepper; brush with teriyaki sauce; turn and repeat. Broil steak 10-12 minutes, turning once; test for desired doneness. Remove steak to cutting board; slice into thin strips. While steak is grilling, in large bowl, mix olive oil, mayonnaise, mustard, lemon juice, garlic and 1 tablespoon parmesan cheese. Add lettuce and cucumber; toss. To serve, place salad mixture on 6 dinner plates. Arrange steak on salad. Sprinkle with remaining parmesan cheese. Serves 6.

*Per serving: 253 calories; 16.6 fat grams*

Foot Note

Chicken, turkey or ham can be substituted for the steak, or used in combination.

# CHICKEN WALDORF SALAD

*This favorite makes great sandwiches with mounds of shredded lettuce.*

2 cups chicken breast or turkey, cooked and
    diced
2 apples, cored and diced
2/3 cup celery, sliced
1/2 cup walnuts, chopped
2/3 cup light mayonnaise
2 tablespoons lemon juice
1/2 teaspoon salt
1/4 teaspoon pepper
Lettuce
Tomato wedges

In large bowl, combine chicken, apples, celery and walnuts. In smaller bowl, mix mayonnaise, lemon juice, salt and pepper. Pour over chicken mixture and toss. Refrigerate. Serve on a salad plate with bed of lettuce and garnish with tomato wedges. Serves 5.

*Per serving: 223 calories; 10.7 fat grams*

 Tuna or turkey can be substituted for the chicken and white or red grapes for the apples.

# GRILLED CHICKEN SALAD WITH FRUIT

*Serve this refreshing salad anytime.  The marinade makes it extra delicious.*

4 chicken breast halves, skinned and
    washed
2 tablespoons olive oil
2 tablespoons balsamic or raspberry vinegar
1 teaspoon Poupon mustard
Salt and pepper to taste
1/2 cup orange juice
6 cups mixed greens
4 peaches, 10 apricots, or 2 cups grapes,
    sliced
1 small red onion, thinly sliced

Prepare chicken.  In small bowl, whisk oil, vinegar, mustard, salt and pepper.  Stir in orange juice, reserving 1/3 cup to use as dressing.  Refrigerate until ready to serve salad.  Place chicken breasts in 8" x 8" baking dish.  Pour juice mixture over chicken and turn to coat both sides.  Cover and refrigerate several hours or overnight.  About 20 minutes before serving time, heat grill or broiler.  Cook chicken about 5 inches above heat 5 minutes on each side.  Check for doneness.  While meat is cooking, prepare salad.  Toss greens, fruit and onions with 1/3 cup reserved dressing.  Divide greens evenly among 6 dinner plates.  Top with chicken and drizzle remaining dressing on top. Serve with warm bread.  Serves 6.

*Per serving: 148 calories; 5.7 fat grams*

# CHINESE CHICKEN SALAD

1/2 large head of cabbage, shredded
4 chicken breasts, cooked and torn or cubed
1 tablespoon onion, chopped
1/2 cup sliced almonds, toasted
4 to 6-ounce package sunflower seed
    kernels
1 package ramen noodles, broken (do not
    use seasoning packet)

Dressing
1/3 cup oil
4 tablespoons water
2 tablespoons sugar
2 tablespoons red wine vinegar
1 1/2 teaspoons pepper

Combine and mix all ingredients, except ramen noodles, in large bowl. Add ramen noodles just before serving. Toss with dressing. Serves 10-12.

Dressing
Combine all ingredients and shake well in container with lid.

*Per serving: 349 calories; 23.2 fat grams*

Chicken breasts can be cooked quickly in the microwave at 60% power (baking mode) 8-12 minutes, rotating every 4 minutes. Cook early and cool in refrigerator.

# CHICKEN ORIENTAL SALAD

*Cyndi dedicates this salad to Sharlene, a friend who lost her life tragically. She was always happy when Cyndi brought it to Christmas gatherings.*

4-6 cooked chicken breast halves, shredded
    or cut up
6 green onions, sliced
4 stalks celery, thinly sliced
1 cup slivered almonds, roasted if desired
1/4 cup sesame seeds, roasted if desired
1 3-ounce package ramen noodles, broken
1/2 head iceberg lettuce, torn

Dressing
4 tablespoons white vinegar
1/2 cup oil
3 teaspoons seasoning salt
1/2 teaspoon pepper
3 tablespoons sugar

Break ramen noodles into bowl with hot water to soften. In large bowl, combine all ingredients. Drain ramen noodles and add to other ingredients. Toss with dressing and serve. Serves 8-10.

Dressing
In container with lid, combine all ingredients. Shake well. Refrigerate until ready to serve salad. Shake again before tossing with salad.

*Per serving: 386 calories; 24.3 fat grams*

# CHICKEN TACO SALAD

1 head lettuce, torn in pieces
4 tortilla bowls
2 cups chicken, cooked and diced
4 green onions, sliced
1/2 cup black olives, halved
1 cup shredded cheddar cheese
1 cup chunky salsa
3/4 cup guacamole
1/2 cup sour cream

Divide lettuce among 4 tortilla bowls. Top with chicken, onions, black olives and cheese. Put mounds of salsa, guacamole and sour cream in each bowl. Serves 4.

*Per serving: 554 calories;  38.0 fat grams*

 Use leftover grilled, baked or fried chicken.

# SHOESTRING SALAD

1 cup chicken, cooked and diced
1 cup celery, diced
1 cup carrots, shredded
1 teaspoon onion flakes
1/2 cup light salad dressing or mayonnaise
1/4 teaspoon prepared mustard
1/2 cup slivered almonds
2 small cans shoestring potatoes

Combine all ingredients, except shoestring potatoes. Just before serving, stir in potatoes. Serves 6.

*Per serving: 187 calories; 11.9 fat grams*

 This salad is excellent served in a tomato.

# TROPICAL CHICKEN SALAD

4 cups cooked chicken, diced
3 tablespoons lemon juice
1 cup celery, sliced
1 teaspoon salt
1/2 teaspoon pepper
1 2-ounce jar pimento, sliced
1/2 cup sliced almonds
1/2 cup light mayonnaise
1 cup seedless grapes, halved
1 cup pineapple chunks, drained

In large bowl, toss chicken with lemon juice. Add remaining ingredients tossing gently until mayonnaise covers all. Serve on lettuce leaves or in a tomato cup with favorite crackers or dinner rolls. Serves 6.

*Per serving: 289 calories; 11.8 fat grams*

 Substitute leftover turkey for chicken.

# SOUTHWESTERN CHICKEN SALAD

*Harriet shared this recipe that was created by her friend, Kathy. Both are excellent cooks.*

6 boneless chicken breast halves, grilled
    and cut into strips
4 cups Romaine lettuce, torn
1 15-ounce can black beans, drained, rinsed
1/2 small red onion, sliced
1/2 cup parmesan cheese
1 cup tortilla chips, coarsly broken

Dressing:
1/4 cup lime juice
1/4 cup olive oil
3 tablespoons cilantro, chopped
1 jalapeño pepper, seeded and chopped

In large bowl, combine chicken, lettuce, beans and onion. Toss with cilantro dressing. Add parmesan cheese and tortilla chips. Toss and serve immediately. Serves 6.

Dressing:
In small bowl, mix ingredients well.

*Per serving: 690 calories; 23.9 fat grams*

# TURKEY FRUIT SALAD

*A delicious salad for the day after Thanksgiving.*

4 cups leftover turkey, cubed
Salt and pepper to taste
1 11-ounce can mandarin oranges, drained
1 cup celery, sliced
1 8-ounce can pineapple tidbits, drained,
    reserving 1 tablespoon juice
6 lettuce leaves

Dressing:
1/2 cup light salad dressing or mayonnaise
1 tablespoon reserved pineapple juice
1/2 teaspoon sugar
1/2 teaspoon dry mustard
1/8 teaspoon salt

In large bowl, season turkey with salt and pepper. Add oranges, celery and pineapple. Cover and chill. Prepare salad dressing. Toss with turkey mixture. On individual salad plates, spoon salad onto lettuce leaves. Serves 6.

Dressing:
In container with lid, combine ingredients; shake well to blend.

*Per serving: 179 calories; 2.9 fat grams*

# HAM AND CHEESE SALAD

*This can be a quick gourmet-looking salad. The cottage cheese mixture is centered on a large serving platter lined on the outer edges with cantaloupe slices.*

1 1/2 cups frozen ham, diced
1 cup fresh green grapes, halved
1 8-ounce can pineapple chunks
1 cup celery, chopped
4 ounces mozzarella cheese, cut in julienne
    strips
2 cups lettuce, torn
Cantaloupe, optional, but great combination
    with salad

Dressing
1 1/2 cups low fat cottage cheese
4 tablespoons chili sauce
2 green onions, chopped
1 1/2 teaspoons basil
Salt and pepper to taste

In large bowl, lightly mix ham, grapes, pineapple, celery and cheese. Refrigerate until ready to serve. Toss with lettuce and half of dressing. Slice cantaloupe thinly and arrange around outside edge of platter. Mound ham mixture in center. Pass salad and remainder of dressing. Serves 6.

Dressing
Place cottage cheese in mixer bowl and beat until almost smooth. Stir in chili sauce, onion, basil, salt and pepper. If possible, make about 2 hours before serving to allow blending of flavors. Refrigerate.

*Per serving: 255 calories; 9.1 fat grams*

# SALMON SALAD

*This combination is also great as a sandwich spread.*

1 15-ounce can pink salmon
1 large onion, chopped
2 stalks celery, sliced
2 tablespoons sweet pickle relish
1/4 cup light mayonnaise
1 teaspoon lemon juice
Salt and pepper to taste
4 cups favorite lettuce, broken
2 tomatoes, wedged

In large bowl, lightly toss salmon, onion, celery and relish. In small bowl, combine mayonnaise, lemon juice, salt and pepper. Toss carefully with salmon mixture. Divide lettuce on separate salad plates. Scoop salmon salad on top. Garnish with tomato wedges. Serves 4.

*Per serving: 201 calories; 7.6 fat grams*

Fresh grilled salmon filets can be substituted for the canned salmon. Lay them on top of remaining ingredients that have been mixed together.

# SHRIMP-PEA SALAD

2 cups frozen peas
1 4 1/2-ounce can shrimp, drained
1/3 cup red pepper, sliced
1/3 cup oil
3 tablespoons red wine vinegar
1/2 teaspoon salt
1/8 teaspoon dried dillweed
Dash pepper
4 cups torn lettuce
2 hard-boiled eggs, sliced

In large bowl, combine peas, shrimp and red pepper. In container with lid, combine oil, vinegar, salt, dillweed and pepper; shake well. Pour over mixture in bowl. Cover and refrigerate several hours. Drain, reserving dressing. Place lettuce in individual salad bowls and top with shrimp-pea mixture. Toss with enough of the reserved dressing to moisten. Garnish with egg slices. Serves 4-6.

*Per serving: 198 calories; 14.3 fat grams*

# SUPER SHRIMP SALAD

1/4 pound lump crab meat
1/4 cup celery, sliced
1/4 cup green pepper, chopped
2 1/2 tablespoons sweet pickle, chopped
3 green onions, finely chopped
1 1/2 teaspoons fresh parsley, minced (or 1
    teaspoon dried parsley)
1/2 cup ripe olives, sliced
1/2 cup pimento stuffed green olives, sliced
1 cup Italian dressing
2 tablespoons olive oil
1 1/2 teaspoons lemon juice
6 lettuce leaves
1 pound large shrimp, cooked
2 tomatoes for garnish

In large airtight container, combine all ingredients except lettuce, shrimp and tomatoes. Store in refrigerator overnight. When ready to serve, line serving platter with lettuce leaves. Spoon salad onto lettuce leaves. Top with shrimp and garnish with tomato wedges. Serves 4-6.

*Per serving: 467 calories; 33 fat grams*

If cooking shrimp, boil in water for 3 to 5 minutes. Drain hot water and rinse in cold water. Peel and devein. Refrigerate until ready to serve.

# TUNA-AVOCADO SALAD

*Especially attractive when served in a tortilla bowl.*

1 head iceberg, Romaine or leaf lettuce,
    torn
1 9 1/4-ounce white tuna in water, broken
    apart
2 tomatoes, cut up
1/2 cup ripe olives, sliced
5-6 green onions, sliced, including tops
1 cup Chinese noodles
1/2 cup cheddar cheese, shredded

Dressing:
1 ripe avocado, mashed
2 tablespoons lemon juice
1/2 cup light sour cream
1/3 cup salad oil
1 clove garlic, crushed
1/2 teaspoon sugar
1/2 teaspoon chili powder
1/4 teaspoon salt
1/4 teaspoon hot pepper sauce

In large bowl, lightly toss all ingredients. Cover with dressing and toss again. Serve on lettuce leaves. Serves 6-8.

Dressing:
In medium bowl, mix all ingredients together well.

*Per serving: 305 calories; 18.7 fat grams*

For a more pungent flavor, substitute curry powder for the chili powder.

For a more hearty meal, serve in small bread bowl. Mix curry, honey and butter together to spread on the extra bread.

# CRAB BED

1-2 heads Romaine lettuce, broken into
    bite-sized pieces
1 pound lump crab meat
4 green onions, sliced, optional
4 tomatoes, quartered
4 hard boiled eggs, quartered
12 ripe or green olives

Dressing:
1 cup bottled chili sauce
3/4 cup light mayonnaise
1 1/2 teaspoons instant minced onion
1 teaspoon sugar
1/2 teaspoon Worcestershire sauce
Salt to taste
Fresh ground pepper to taste

Place lettuce on six salad plates.  Crumble crab
meat on top.  Sprinkle onions and arrange tomatoes
and eggs on top.  Garnish with 2 or 3 olives.  Serve
dressing on the side.  Refrigerate until ready to
serve.  Serves 6.

Dressing:
In medium bowl, mix all ingredients.  Cover and
chill until ready to serve salad.

*Per serving: 185 calories; 6.6 fat grams*

 Canned crab meat and bottled dressing can be used.

*Salads*
Page 143

# TABOULI

1 1/2 cups bulgur wheat
2 cups boiling water
2 tomatoes, chopped
1 stalk celery, diced
1 bunch green onions, chopped
1 cucumber, chopped
1 green pepper, chopped
1 carrot, diced
1/2 cup oil
1/2 cup lemon juice
Salt and pepper to taste

In large bowl, combine bulgur wheat and boiling water. Allow to set 30 minutes. Mix in remaining ingredients and chill until ready to serve. Serves 6-8.

*Per serving: 272 calories; 16.2 fat grams*

 Use the blender or food processor to chop the vegetables for quicker preparation.

# CURRIED RICE SALAD

*This is a great way to use leftover rice.*

1 cup long-grain rice, cooked
1/2 cup celery, chopped
1/4 cup green onions, chopped
1/4 red pepper, chopped
2 tablespoons slivered almonds, toasted
1/4 fat free Italian dressing
1 teaspoon white vinegar
1/2 teaspoon curry powder

In medium bowl, combine first 5 ingredients. In small bowl, blend dressing, vinegar and curry powder; add to rice mixture and toss. Cover and chill. Serves 4.

*Per serving: 207 calories; 2.8 fat grams*

# HOT VEGETABLE AND RICE SALAD

*A touch of the south for those who love okra.  Great as a hot salad, and just as good the next day served cold.*

3 cups cooked rice (cook while preparing
    rest of salad)
4 slices bacon, cooked crisp and crumbled
2 tablespoons bacon drippings
1 onion, chopped
1/2 green pepper, chopped
1 cup fresh or frozen okra, sliced
2 tomatoes, chopped
1/2 teaspoon salt
1/4 teaspoon pepper

In large skillet, saute onion and green pepper in bacon drippings until barely tender.  Add okra, tomatoes, salt and pepper and cook 5 minutes.  Add rice.  Cook 15 minutes or until liquid is absorbed.  Stir bacon into mixture.  Remove to large bowl and serve immediately.  Serves 8.

*Per serving: 316 calories; 5.4 fat grams*

# CHICKEN RICE SALAD

1 6-ounce package chicken-flavored rice
    mix, prepared as directed, cooled
1 6-ounce jar marinated artichoke hearts,
    drained and reserved
2 green onions, chopped
1/2 green pepper, chopped
1/4 cup green olives, sliced
1 cup fresh mushrooms, sliced

Dressing:
1/2 cup light mayonnaise
Marinade from artichokes
1/2-1 teaspoon curry powder

In large bowl, combine all ingredients. Carefully
toss with dressing. Chill well. Serves 10-12.

Dressing:
In small bowl, mix all ingredients.

*Per serving: 90 calories; 1.1 fat grams*

# SHRIMP AND MACARONI SALAD

*When Cyndi lived in San Diego, a friend and co-worker would be the hit of any gathering when she brought this salad.*

2 cups elbow macaroni
1 onion
1/2 green pepper
3-4 stalks celery
3 dill pickles
1/2 cup stuffed green olives, sliced
2 6-ounce cans large deveined shrimp

Dressing
1 1/2 cups light salad dressing or light mayonnaise
2 teaspoons prepared mustard
2 dashes hot pepper sauce
1 teaspoon seasoned salt
1/2 teaspoon pepper
1 hard-boiled egg, chopped finely

Cook macaroni according to package directions. Rinse in cold water. While macaroni is cooking, chop onion, pepper, celery and pickles in blender or food processor. Combine with macaroni. Add olives and shrimp. Prepare dressing and mix lightly. Serves 6-8.

Dressing
In medium bowl, mix all ingredients together.

*Per serving: 256 calories; 6 fat grams*

# BLUE CHEESE PASTA SALAD

*For blue cheese lovers, Carol adds a favorite to this pasta dish.*

1 8-ounce package spiral pasta, cooked
    according to package directions
4 ounces blue cheese
1 6-ounce can black olives, sliced
2 bunches green onions, sliced
1 2-ounce small roll hard salami, sliced or
    cut into pieces
1 cup light mayonnaise

In large bowl, combine all ingredients and lightly toss.  Serves 6-8.

*Per serving: 272 calories; 11.2 fat grams*

 Vary this salad with different shapes and flavors of pasta.

# HEARTY SHRIMP AND HAM PASTA SALAD

*There are so many good things in this salad that it is a great hot main meal entree.*

1 8-ounce package spiral or pinwheel pasta,
    cooked and drained
1 garlic clove, minced
1/4 teaspoon ground ginger
1 tablespoon olive oil
1 pound fresh asparagus, trimmed and cut
    in bite-sized pieces
1/2 pound uncooked shrimp, peeled and
    deveined
2 tablespoons water
3 slices ham, julienned
1 8-ounce can water chestnuts, sliced
1/2 cup celery, sliced
1/3 cup ripe olives, sliced

Dressing:
6 tablespoons oil
2 tablespoons cider vinegar
1 tablespoon soy sauce
1/8 teaspoon dry mustard
1 teaspoon brown sugar
Salt and pepper to taste

Cook pasta and keep warm. In large skillet, cook garlic, ginger, oil, asparagus, shrimp and water about 10 minutes. Stir in ham, water chestnuts and olives. Heat 2 minutes. Place hot pasta in large bowl; add shrimp mixture. Toss with dressing. Serve immediately. Serves 4-6.

Dressing:
In container with lid, combine all ingredients. Cover and shake well to mix.

*Per serving: 422 calories; 21.9 fat grams*

# TORTELLINI PASTA SALAD

*These little cheese-filled pastas are great in salads. A selection can be found in the freezer section or the dried pasta area of the grocery store.*

1 16-ounce package cheese-filled tortellini, cooked, drained, cooled
1/2 cup roasted red peppers, drained, cut in thin strips
1/2 cup green pepper, chopped
1/2 cup red onion, coarsely chopped
1/2 cup frozen peas
1/2 cup black olives, sliced
1/4 cup parmesan cheese
1 cup light ranch dressing
Alfalfa sprouts

In large bowl, combine all ingredients, except alfalfa sprouts. Toss to coat pasta. Refrigerate until ready to serve. Line salad plates or bowl with alfalfa sprouts. Spoon salad on top. Serves 6-8.

*Per serving: 268 calories; 9.4 fat grams*

Serve with a side of frosted grapes, allowing enough time for them to dry.

Frosted Grapes:
Wash 2 bunches of red and/or white grapes and dry well. Separate into clusters. Brush grapes with egg white, slightly beaten and roll in 1/2-3/4 cup sugar to coat. Place on wire rack to dry for about 1 hour.

# PISTACHIO SALAD

1 20-ounce can crushed pineapple, drained, reserving juice
1 small package pistachio pudding
1 9-ounce container whipped topping
1 cup miniature marshmallows
1/2 cup pecans or walnuts, finely chopped

In large bowl, combine 4 tablespoons pineapple juice with pudding mix. Stir enough to make a smooth paste. Add pineapple, whipped topping, marshmallows and chopped nuts. Mix well until mixture is fluffy and increased in volume. Refrigerate until thoroughly chilled. Serve as salad or dessert. Serves 8-10.

*Per serving: 170 calories; 5.8 fat grams*